CU00704395

# BEYOND THE CHILDREN'S CORNER

### Creating a culture of welcome for all ages

## Margaret Pritchard Houston

## With an Afterword by Sandra Millar

CHURCH HOUSE
PUBLISHING

Church House Publishing
Church House
Great Smith Street
London SW1P 3AZ

ISBN 978 1 78140 164 4

Published 2020 by Church House Publishing
Copyright © Margaret Pritchard Houston 2020

All rights reserved. No part of this publication may be reproduced, or stored or transmitted by any means or in any form, electronic or mechanical, including photocopying, recording, or any information storage or retrieval system without written permission which should be sought from the Copyright Administrator, Church House Publishing, Church House, Great Smith Street, London SW1P 3AZ.

Email: copyright@churchofengland.org

The author has asserted her right under the Copyright, Designs and Patents Act, 1988, to be identified as the author of this Work.

The opinions expressed in this book are those of the author and do not necessarily reflect the official policy of the General Synod or The Archbishops' Council of the Church of England.

Scripture quotations are from New Revised Standard Version Bible: Anglicized Edition, copyright © 1989, 1995 National Council of the Churches of Christ in the United States of America. Used by permission. All rights reserved worldwide.

Typeset by Regent Typesetting
Printed and bound in England by
CPI Group (UK) Ltd

# Contents

# Introduction

Then I said, 'Ah, Lord GOD! Truly I do not know how to speak, for I am only a boy.' But the LORD said to me,
'Do not say, "I am only a boy";
for you shall go to all to whom I send you,
and you shall speak whatever I command you.
Do not be afraid of them,
for I am with you to deliver you,
says the LORD.'
*Jeremiah 1.6–8*

*Once upon a time, there was a beautiful, safe place where everyone was happy. People lived together in harmony, and were positive about the future. Then, something changed, and the community became desolated – instead of living in the beautiful, safe place, the people found themselves cast out into the desert, in exile from what felt like 'home', and fearful about what was happening next.*

Sound familiar?

It's the beginning of almost every fairy tale in history. It's similar to the narrative of the first three chapters of Genesis. And it's the story many of our churches tell themselves about their history.

That perceived 'golden age' ended in the 1960s, when the real fall-off in church attendance, especially among children and

young people, began. As a diocesan advisor, I meet with many
PCCs and leadership teams and, when I ask them to tell me
the story of children and families in their churches, it usually
begins with 'We used to have lots of children and young people,
and then …'

There is usually a sense of longing and a sense of anxiety behind
these words. Longing for what used to be – for a time when
our church community felt like it was thriving, a time when we
had a sense of invigorating new life in our pews, a confidence
that the faith that mattered to us would live on after us in the
children who were being raised in it. And there is anxiety – fear
that our churches will close, that our communities will cease to
exist, that the faith that feeds us will die. And fear that children
and young people are losing out on what we ourselves have had
– the support of a church community, the sense of belonging we
gain from it, and a faith in Jesus that provides a framework of
meaning and hope for our lives.

We are standing in the desert, banging on the closed door of
Eden, trying to get back in.

Here's the bad news: we can't.

Here's the good news: the golden age probably wasn't as good as
we remember it being.

There are many books on the reasons behind the decades-long
decline in church attendance numbers, and I won't try to re-create
them here. Suffice to say that for many, the church served as a
cultural institution rather than a place of worship. As Andrew
Brown wrote in *The Guardian*, 'Anglicans generally have never
been fervent believers. [It is just that] they are now being
replaced by children and grandchildren who are unfervent

nonbelievers.'[1] Nobody would be keen about our pews being full of people who were there simply because cultural norms expected them to be – that isn't the Kingdom of God.

The full pews we saw as a sign of hope and a widespread love of Jesus may, in fact, have been illusory. And what we are seeing now – a dedicated small number of believers, a large and uncertain fringe – may be a more accurate reflection of how the country has felt towards the Church for a long time. What we have lost may not have been a large community of believers, but the sense of church being 'just what people do'.

And this means we have opportunities: the opportunity to grow because we are *attractive*, not because we are *expected*; the opportunity to build a community that genuinely serves the needs of all of God's children in our parishes, not one that is full of a few believers and a larger number of people who are there simply because it's what everyone expects of you on a Sunday morning. More recently, the coronavirus outbreak of 2020 also forced us into changing how we do worship, outreach, ministry and service, and showed us new opportunities and possibilities.

Then he said to me, 'Mortal, these bones are the whole house of Israel. They say, "Our bones are dried up, and our hope is lost; we are cut off completely." Therefore prophesy, and say to them, Thus says the Lord God: I am going to open your graves, and bring you up from your graves, O my people; and I will bring you back to the land of Israel. And you shall know that I am the Lord, when I open your graves, and bring you up from your graves, O my people. I will put my spirit within you, and you shall live, and I will place you on your own soil;

---

1 Brown, Andrew, 'No Religion is the New Religion', *The Guardian*, 20 January 2016, www.theguardian.com/commentisfree/2016/jan/20/no-religion-britons-atheism-christianity.

then you shall know that I, the LORD, have spoken and will act, says the LORD.'
*Ezekiel 37.11–14*

The story of God's people is one of loss and renewal, over and over. It is a story of dry bones living again, of water breaking out in the desert, of life coming out of death. While the people are despairing in Babylon, that 'our bones are dried up, and our hope is lost', God is promising renewal and rebuilding. He is promising a homecoming, a renewed sense of identity. The people of God do indeed return home after their exile in Babylon. And the children and youth hear God's story read to them in the ruins of the Temple, for the first time.

But God doesn't create renewal alone. God needs us to do the work alongside him. And for renewal and new life to happen, many of our churches need to change. This can feel difficult sometimes – but we do have the power to do it. We need to change our churches into places that have a culture of welcome, places where children and those who care for them are accepted, nurtured, taken seriously and given what they need to flourish spiritually.

Very few churches truly believe they're unwelcoming. But the thing is, our own churches and communities are so familiar to us that sometimes we can have trouble seeing the ways we might, without meaning to, be getting in the way of welcoming new people, especially children.

# What is Meant by 'a Culture of Welcome'?

Culture is defined as 'the ideas, customs and social behaviour of a particular people or society'. Often, like a fish that doesn't know water is wet, the people who exist within a culture don't see it. It's just normal to them.

When I moved to the UK in 2005, I realized everyone talked about the weather. A lot. I realized that talking about the weather was often the gateway to a proper conversation – you would talk about the weather and then move on to other topics, and that's how you got to know someone.

I tried to join in with conversations about the weather, but they always stalled. I was a bit baffled. A German friend told me to read the anthropologist Kate Fox's book *Watching the English*, a hilarious and deeply insightful look at English culture. I realized I had been talking about the weather wrong – in the USA, where I come from, talking about the weather is a competitive activity. 'Oh, you think *this* is hot, well, when I was camping in Arizona last year, it was 120 degrees Fahrenheit every day and it hadn't rained for two hundred years!' 'This hurricane? It's nothing. Let me tell you about the tornado we had back in 89!' And so on. But Fox says the first rule English people follow when talking about the weather is *you always have to agree with what's just been said.* If someone says, 'It's hot!', you have to say, 'Yes, it *is* hot, isn't it?' Once I figured this out, I found it much easier to make friends and get to know people.

I tell this story to my English friends now, and they usually pause, laugh, and go, 'Wow, that *is* how we talk about the weather. I never noticed that. And yes, the competitive approach *would* put us off!'

The fish don't know water is wet. Our own culture is often invisible to us.

Every denomination and every individual church has its own set of ideas, customs and social behaviour. These may or may not be ones that create a place where children and families are safe and welcome – *even if the church thinks they are.*

We don't realize that many of these ideas, customs and social behaviours are getting in the way – our unspoken assumptions about who worship is for, about the role of children in worship, about how children 'should' behave, about how we organize and use our space, about how we view children and their spiritual development. We think 'Oh yes, we'd love to have some children on Sundays', and think that means we're a welcoming church – but there's a lot more to it than that. (Though that is a brilliant start, and if you actively *don't* want children on Sunday, then you have a harder road ahead.)

Changing a culture means changing the prevailing, often invisible, ideas, customs and social behaviour. That is the process this book will hopefully help you with, by encouraging you to examine your church's invisible culture, identify the ways in which you may be inhibiting families from feeling welcome, and by helping you to change that in a way that doesn't lead to World War Three among your congregation.

There is, of course, no one right answer and no one right way. Every community is different. That's why this book has more case studies, discussion questions and interviews than it has lists of dos and don'ts. Hopefully, by seeing what others have

## A few elements of culture[2]

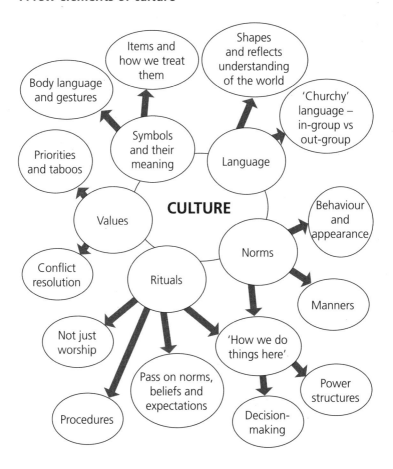

Body language and gestures

Items and how we treat them

Shapes and reflects understanding of the world

'Churchy' language – in-group vs out-group

Priorities and taboos

Symbols and their meaning

Language

Values

**CULTURE**

Behaviour and appearance

Conflict resolution

Norms

Rituals

Manners

Not just worship

'How we do things here'

Procedures

Pass on norms, beliefs and expectations

Decision-making

Power structures

done, and what parents, children and church leaders have to say about their experiences, you'll be able to see your own church in a new light and figure out your own way forward.

2 From Barkan, Steven E., *Sociology: Brief Edition*, Ch. 2, 'The Elements of Culture', University of Minnesota, 2012. Available via Creative Commons at https://2012books.lardbucket.org/books/sociology-brief-edition-v1.1/s05-02-the-elements-of-culture.html.

At times, this book may start to feel overwhelming or even discouraging. You may feel that you're a long way from where you want to be, you're burned out and you have the nagging suspicion that every other church in the world is doing better than you are. From my own experiences in ministry, and from talking to dozens of others, I think we *all* feel that way.

Remember, you do not have to do everything in this book. And you definitely don't have to do it all by next week. As they say in 12-step fellowships – take what works, and leave the rest. And take it one day at a time.

## Remember Why this Matters

We hear so often how important it is to be a welcoming – and inviting – and missional – church. We hear how important children and families are. It can be helpful to remember *why* it's important.

It's easy to get lost in panic about declining numbers and pressure from outside about posting figures of growth (especially among children and young people). But if we focus on those as our reasons for wanting to welcome children and families, then we're focusing on the negative. We're focusing on anxiety. That doesn't help to motivate, refresh or energize people.

We may also, if we're honest, feel pressure to make our churches appear successful – to ourselves and others – by having lots of happy children who are enthusiastic about coming to church. It makes us feel good. But, again, that focuses on appearances and pressure, not on love.

And neither of these truly create a culture of *welcome*. Focusing on external pressure creates a culture of anxiety. Focusing on wanting to feel and look successful can create a culture of pandering and insecurity. What we really want to be doing is creating a culture of welcome, love and inclusion, a community of all ages worshipping and learning about God together.

Because that's the real reason we're doing this – love. And remembering that will help focus us, sustain us and motivate us. God is a God of love, and wants to love everyone. And church is God's house, not ours. So if we have turned church into a place where the culture is such that children don't feel welcome, we are getting between them and God's love. Jesus had some pretty harsh words for that.[3] If we think the gospel is good news, if it's the thing we hold on to when life threatens to overwhelm us, if it's the thing that gives us hope and meaning, if it's where we find unconditional love, then sharing it with children is giving them a gift.

And if our communities live out the gospel, then our communities become the embodiment of that gift. They become a place where all are welcome, all are loved, all are safe and all are invited to take the water of life without price. And in our society, that is rare and precious.

Sally Nash, Director of the Midlands Institute for Children, Youth and Mission, writes, 'In an era of cuts in public spending on children, in the UK at least, it may be that the Church is the only institution in some communities offering open-access provision for children and young people. It is also one that can offer a long-term presence, and while employed clergy and

---

3 Matthew 18.5-6.

workers may come and go, there are usually people within the congregation who offer a continuity of presence and welcome.'[4]

We have the chance to be something genuinely countercultural – because the Kingdom of God is radical. Peter Ormerod writes that 'an effective church can offer comfort and reassurance, emphasizing that everyone is loved, and is of the same inherent value, just as they are. It's not about perfect selfies and Instagram likes and exam grades and money and status.'[5] Church may be the one place where children and teenagers hear this message – and that matters.

# Welcome to Church, Welcome Home

What does it mean to be welcome, and at home, somewhere? I asked several teens and pre-teens who have grown up in the church where I served as the children's worker. Here are some of their answers:

'When you first meet me, and in general, in big groups of people I don't know, I can be quite shy and don't talk much. So for me, somewhere I belong is where I feel comfortable talking to people and can be quite chatty. And where I don't mind if what I say is wrong, where you're free to make mistakes and not be judged for it – you can be comfortable and enjoy your time with people.'
*Mary, aged 16*

---

4 Nash, Sally, *Re-thinking Children's Work in Churches: A Practical Guide*, London and Philadelphia, PA: Jessica Kingsley Publishers, 2019, p. 12.

5 www.theguardian.com/commentisfree/2018/mar/22/christianity-norm-underground-mystery.

'Where I feel at home is where I don't have to try. I don't have to always be alert to what I'm saying or what I'm doing – I can just relax.'
*Matilda, aged 14*

'With some friends, you feel like you always have to be doing something, but with your closer friends, you normally feel like you don't have to be doing something, you can just be lying down and talking, and that makes you feel like you belong, because you're speaking to them, you're not trying too hard, you can just be yourself.'
*Delilah, aged 12*

'Diversity is really important. And to be honest, this church isn't … unbelievably diverse … but age-wise, there is a lot of diversity. And it's nice. And there's something about older people that I really like. I think they're wise. There's something about security, around older people, that I really love.'
*Jess, aged 17*

Over and over, we hear that what matters to children and young people is not knowing the latest music or having a cool young pastor, but authenticity, community, relationships and acceptance. A place where you can 'make mistakes and not be judged for it', a place where you can 'feel comfortable', where you can 'just be lying down and talking', a place where you have the 'security' Jess talks about, of being part of an intergenerational community and knowing you belong.

This is the role a church can play in the life of a young family now – a community of all ages who will love and support you and your child.

Church can be a place where you are not assessed and tested, but can simply *be*. Where your identity comes not from your marks, or your likes on Instagram, but from being a beloved child of God.

A gospel that tells you over and over that God loves you 'to the moon and back',[6] no matter what.

Church can be a place where we can be real together, and share our lives.

A community that speaks out into the world the radical truth that all people – no matter their age, abilities, gender, skin colour, income or anything else – are loved and accepted by God, and should be treated with dignity.

This is what we can be, once we stop mourning for what we may never have been. This is what many churches are already becoming.

So this is the even better news: the future might be *even better* than the past. If we can let go of our longing for Eden, we can set our sights on the Kingdom. It's certainly better than standing in the desert, facing backwards, and banging on a closed door.

---

6 This is from the children's book *Guess How Much I Love You* by Sam McBratney (London: Walker, 2014), which has fabulous parallels to the gospel – a father hare playfully competing with his son to express how much they love each other. The baby finishes by saying, 'I love you to the moon.' The dad waits until his son is asleep and says, 'I love you to the moon … and back.' It would make a great baptism gift for families, and is also used in the programme *Starting Rite* by Jenny Paddison (London: Church House Publishing, 2015), which is a series of six sessions for parents and babies together, exploring spirituality through play and conversation.

Also, if the best thing is for churches to be places of authentic worship, service and community, then that means that we don't need to turn them into funfairs to attract children, or into nightclubs to attract young people. This may be the best news of all – that what we value, at all ages, is pretty much the same. To attract children and families, you don't need to transform your worship and your community out of all recognition to your older members. It's not a zero-sum game. You will still be yourself, the community you are now – just different.

It's difficult, and you won't always be able to please everyone. But this book can hopefully help you manage that process of change as well as possible, and provide a worship environment that is nurturing of the faith of children and families, as well as others. There are some common mistakes, and if you avoid these you are more likely to provide a process of change that brings people along instead of alienates them, that is reflective of Kingdom values and not anxiety-fuelled flailing.

## Facing the Anxiety – And Moving On

It's tough to avoid anxiety sometimes, especially when reading national statistics around children's church attendance. The Church of England Statistics for Mission for 2017 show a median of three under-16s in church each week – either on Sunday or in a weekday service or Fresh Expression. This means 50% of Church of England churches have three or fewer children in a church service every week. A quarter of churches have none at all. Even the top 25% of churches report 11 children attending each week, on average.[7] The average Methodist church has

---

7 www.churchofengland.org/sites/default/files/2018-11/2017Statistics ForMission_007_.pdf, p. 9.

six people under the age of 20 attending services each week, including both Sunday and weekday visits.[8]

And yet one in ten children across England have a Church of England christening before their first birthday. The 'Baptism Matters' research done by the Church of England's Life Events team shows that when you add toddlers being baptized, this number rises to one in six. And that's only one denomination. It's difficult to pin down exact numbers on baby and toddler groups, as many of these fly under the radar, but research suggests more than half of churches in England run them. So there is still extensive and widespread contact with families in the first few years of their children's lives.

These scary-sounding statistics are often not the whole story. Many of those parishes reporting next to no children may be in a benefice with a parish that has thriving children's ministry, and families from all around the benefice are provided with a nurturing community in that one parish. So a list of four parishes, where three have no children on a Sunday, may in fact be succeeding at ministering with families from all four parishes through that fourth church.

Meanwhile, many churches are successfully forming relation-ships with children and families in other ways. Projects like Open the Book[9] and Worship Workshop[10] encourage and enable schools to be places where children hear the stories of the

---

8 Methodist Statistics for Mission don't contain this exact value, so I took the total number of October visits on page 3 and divided it by the total number of churches on page 4. Since the vast majority of Methodist churches are small or very small, the median number of young people each week will be significantly smaller than this average; www.methodist.org.uk/media/8615/infographics_2018_final.pdf.

9 www.biblesociety.org.uk/get-involved/open-the-book/.

10 https://worshipworkshop.org.uk/.

Bible and worship together, while Messy Church[11] and other initiatives have provided space for creative worship, art, table fellowship and more, in family-friendly ways.

A parish in my diocese was recently lamenting their lack of contact with children because they have none on Sunday mornings. 'We do have an Open the Book team, though', they said, 'So I suppose that's something.' A few questions later, and I discovered that through this one parish, a total of 600 children are encountering a Bible story in school every week. And yet they feel like they're failing, because few children arrive on Sunday morning.

Another parish with an average of two children a week has a monthly family service with ten children and their carers on a Sunday afternoon. Another has a weekly toddler group, with a Bible story and worship, for 10–20 children, plus parents and grandparents – a genuine intergenerational Christian community. And many of these children appear nowhere in our official statistics. They are invisible.

These ministries are often discounted, even by the people who run them. They are often seen as a consolation prize for not having children on Sunday morning. But they are real and vital, especially now, when so many families are involved in sports on Sunday morning and won't make it to your normal service.

However, sometimes they're set up as a way of trying to sidestep making cultural change: 'Our Sunday service is really unwelcoming, but we can set up a Messy Church and get to children that way.' But even that will ultimately probably get you into trouble. Your Sunday service will need to support and value

11 www.messychurch.org.uk/.

your Messy Church, or your teatime family service, or your Open the Book ministry. They will need to pray for it. They may need to help fund it, at the beginning at least. They will need to agree to volunteer for it, maybe to share your space with it, and ideally create relationships and a shared sense of community between their congregation and your more family-orientated one – and they will need to welcome any families who decide to jump from one to the other, or to come on Sunday morning to see the people who do Open the Book at their kid's school.

So setting up something outside Sunday morning isn't necessarily a way to avoid trying to change the culture of your existing congregation. If you decide to set up something outside Sunday morning, it needs to be done because it's the right thing to do, in your particular context, not just because your Sunday service isn't a good place for families to come.

Even with the wonderful variety of ways that churches are finding to reach out to children and families, Sunday morning still matters. It is the easiest way for us all to worship together, to create an intergenerational Christian community. One of the most common challenges with family-specific programmes is when children 'age out' of them, and the church isn't able to provide a complete age 0–25 pathway of programmes. Sunday morning is that pathway – we're all there together, 0–100 and beyond.

Sunday morning is, in many places, Eucharistic, with a Communion service at least once a month in most denominations and parishes. It is a place where we come together to share Christ's body and his blood, to live out the story of Christ's salvation of the world, week after week. This is a powerful experience. The 'Rooted in the Church' report found that a very high number of young adults who stayed in the church through adolescence had been admitted to communion before confirmation.[12] Sunday morning is also an important aspect of what anthropologists call 'enculturation' – the process by which an individual takes on the norms and culture of a group and makes being a member of that group part of their own identity. By learning what churches do in 'normal' worship (whatever that is), with all of us together, children learn what the group does, and that they belong to it.

So whether or not your church has meaningful ministries with children and families at other times, it is worth considering what changes can be made to make your Sunday services more welcoming to children and families.

This book is intended as a guide to accompany you on that process. It relies extensively on my own experiences as a diocesan children's work advisor and as a parish children's and families worker, but also on interviews, research and writings by others.

- First, we take a look at the modern family, to gain a better understanding of the lives of those people we are trying to reach.
- From there, we look at how you can make the most of the resources already present in your church, and at what changes can be made to the space in order to enable children to engage more easily with worship.
- Then we look at many of the common barriers to welcoming children and families, the hidden and unspoken assumptions and dynamics behind them, and some ways of changing the culture.
- Finally, we look at what it really means to fully welcome children – as fellow disciples and decision-makers.

---

12 www.churchofengland.org/sites/default/files/2017-11/Rooted%20 in%20the%20Church%20Summary%20Report.pdf.

# A Note About Safeguarding

Throughout this book, I repeatedly discuss the importance of relationships. The ability for church members to form relationships with one another is crucial for a welcoming community. From people who serve as greeters, to people who could be on 'cuddle duty' for babies, to baptism buddies and more, bringing the congregation as a whole into relationship with each other, and with children and their carers, matters.

All of this needs to be done in a culture that values safeguarding. Safeguarding is not a box-ticking exercise – it is crucial for mission and ministry. If the relationships children and their carers form at church are not safe, it will affect how they think about the church, how they think about Christians and, most importantly, how they think about God. If we do not respond well as an institution when concerns are raised, they will lose trust in us, and in the God we claim to serve. Make sure that people who volunteer to take on significant roles with children and families are checked, and that people know who they can report concerns to. Ensure that leadership – including volunteer leaders – have regular safeguarding training. Use Safer Recruitment for volunteers as well as paid staff. And talk to your parish safeguarding officer or diocesan safeguarding advisor if you don't know what this means, or if you have any questions or concerns.[13]

The NSPCC also has a helpline where you can talk to an expert if you're not sure how to proceed with a situation that concerns you, and Childline has posters available so children who come to your church are made aware of it.

---

13 The Church of England's safeguarding policy and practice guidance can be found online at www.churchofengland.org/safeguarding.

If your church has a difficult track record with Safeguarding, or there have been historical problems that still hang over the community, then changing the culture to one that welcomes Safeguarding and acknowledges its importance is crucial before you can truly be a place of welcome for children and families.

# Acknowledgements

Thanks first and foremost to all at Church House Publishing who believed this book was important, and took it on.

This book would not exist without the dozens of clergy, Readers, children's workers, lay leaders of worship, PCC members, churchwardens and volunteers in the Diocese of St Albans, who invited me to their churches and allowed me to accompany them on their journeys, whether for a day or for many years. And it would not exist without my fellow diocesan children's and youth advisors, who shared their stories and experiences. And it would not exist without the wisdom of Dean Pusey and Julie Cirillo, who have unfailingly supported children and young people and those who minister with them.

Thanks are also due to the Revd Ruth Pyke, my predecessor at St Albans, and the work she did before me, especially with the Core Skills course and the toolkit for churches with few or no children, and to the Revds Tim Lomax and Kate Peacock, and my colleagues in the Mission and Ministry departments.

Thanks also to the parents who let me interview their children for this book, and to the children themselves. Thank you to the clergy, lay ministers, volunteers and parents who spoke to me either in person or online and shared what were often difficult or painful experiences. And to the Revds Lizzi Green and Ally Barrett, who read the first draft and offered very helpful feedback.

But this book especially wouldn't exist without the clergy and people of St George's Church in Campden Hill, who took me on in 2010 as a keen new children's worker with a lot of ideas but very little finesse, and helped me find the way. Thanks especially to the Revds Michael Fuller, Robert Thompson, James Heard, Peter Wolton and Neil Traynor, and also to Clare Heard, Martina Sadovska, Bill James, Minh Tam Janssens, Becky Barrow, Tilly Culme-Seymour, Shy Robson and so many more. And thank you to all the children who have passed through the doors of St George's over the years, for teaching me so much about God.

Some names and identifying details in case studies have been changed. Quotes from discussions have occasionally been paraphrased from my memory of a conversation. Quotes from interviews are replicated verbatim.

# 1

# We Are Family

When you hear the word 'family', what image springs immediately to mind?

Despite the fact that most of us know better, the image that probably came to you was of a heterosexual couple in their twenties or thirties, with a few young children. They may be well dressed and smiling. They might have a dog.

This might bear no relation to your family now, or the family you grew up in, yet it's still the prevailing archetype of family. But more and more, modern families reflect a broader and more diverse vision of family. While that may make us nervous, actually a diversity of family styles – and families who struggle and have problems and can't always stay together – is very biblical. For better or worse, family has never been simple and straightforward. And God's welcome to families, the families God chooses to work with and make holy, is broader than just the nuclear family. And more complicated.

The families in the Bible include polygamy, the use of a woman's servant as a surrogate for pregnancy without the servant's consent, the ostracism of women with infertility, the command for a rape victim to marry their abuser, and more.

And there are stories that are universal in how they show the painful and broken sides of family life – one of the first family stories of the Bible, that of Cain and Abel, is one of murderous sibling rivalry and jealousy.

Isaac blatantly favours one son over another, and this sin has long-term consequences – estrangement, exile, loss. Only when the brothers can begin to trust each other, to stop fighting over scraps of their father's love, can reconciliation occur.

Rachel and Leah are bought and sold as property by their cousin, and their relationship is one of bitterness and envy, vying for position. Absalom rises in armed rebellion against his father, and their feud brings a whole country into bloodshed.

Yet these flawed men and women, who hurt each other and break relationships, are people of God. Any theology of family must reckon with this, must have a place for those whose family relationships aren't picture-perfect. But it must do this without excusing damage and abuse or demanding immediate forgiveness without justice and atonement for the real hurt caused.

On the other side of this coin, however, there are places in the Bible where God urges his people to understand that family is more than blood, and that the love of family is broader than the stereotypical nuclear family with 2.4 kids and a pet.

Ruth, an outsider and immigrant, is brought into the family of God through her care for her late husband's mother, and becomes an ancestor of King David and Jesus. Samuel is given by his mother to the Temple, and raised (fostered?) by Eli, whose relationship with his own sons is troubled, at best.

Jesus is raised by his biological mother and a stepfather, and later says that anyone who follows him is his sibling, regardless of whether they are his blood relatives. On the cross, he gives Mary and the Beloved Disciple to each other, as mother and son.

And the early Church was suspicious of marriage and parenting, encouraging Christians instead to prepare themselves for the coming of the Kingdom.

Any understanding our churches have of family must therefore also be broader than blood relations, and account for different kinds of relationships and structures of family – as well as for those who choose, or by circumstance are made, to live without a family.

This is because ultimately, in baptism, we are called to a non-hierarchical family, 'children of the same heavenly Father', all one generation apart from God himself. We are all family because we are children of God.

---

### Reflection

Take a few minutes to write down all the different household configurations, of two or more people, that you might encounter in your parish.

Which of these have grown significantly in the last 50 years?

What makes a family?

Why did God make families?

What is different about family life now from 50 years ago?

---

Now take a look at your list of different household configurations above, and compare it to the list below.

# Who Are Family?

The *We Are Family* research conducted by the Methodist Church found that church workers reported coming into contact with many different kinds of families, including:

- Two-parent heterosexual families;
- Single-parent families;
- Couples without children;
- Same-sex couples with children;
- Families from a range of ethnic groups;
- Fostering and adoptive families;
- Blended families, with step-parents and step-children;
- Families with additional-needs children;
- Extended families, involving different generations;
- Couples whose children have left home;
- Families with a carer.[14]

Are there any on your list that are missing from the one above?

Even within these groups, there is variation. A foster family may be fostering children biologically related to one or more of the parents, or not. A single parent family may be a woman who had fertility treatment on her own, a widow or widower raising their children, or a parent who has divorced. A two-parent family may be legally married or cohabiting. Same-sex couples may be raising children from previous heterosexual relationships, so they may also be a blended family, or they may be raising children conceived together through fertility treatment or adopted children.

---

14 *We Are Family: The Changing Face of Family Ministry*, London: Methodist Publishing (updated edition, 2017), p. 9.

Couples without children may be waiting until the time is right, or they may have chosen not to have children. They may be undergoing fertility treatment and longing for a child. They may be bereaved parents, their status as parents visible only to themselves and those who know of their loss.

But while there is a great deal of variation in types and structures of family, the Office for National Statistics found in 2016 that married or civil-partnered families are still the most common type, though cohabiting unmarried couples are the fastest growing.[15] The majority of children still grow up in households with two parents – though of course some of these may be blended families, or have children with additional needs, or otherwise fit one of the other categories listed above.

What services are there for families in your area? What types of families do they serve? What fostering and adoption services are nearby? Are there children's centres? Mental health services? A children's hospital? A fertility clinic? A foodbank? What different configurations of families are living in your area and what are their needs?

Because despite a strong cultural narrative of modern life being more isolated than ever before, the idea that 'it takes a village to raise a child' still resonates with parents, and the church is part of that village. The research into baptisms conducted by the Church of England's Life Events team found that the biggest reason for parents wanting their children to be baptized was so that they would have godparents.[16]

---

15 www.ons.gov.uk/peoplepopulationandcommunity/birthsdeaths andmarriages/families/bulletins/familiesandhouseholds/2016.

16 Church of England Life Events; https://churchsupporthub.org/ baptisms/explore-thinking/importance-godparents/.

'A christening gives parents the opportunity to formally involve other significant adults in their child's upbringing, for advice, protection, support and encouragement, and they will give a lot of thought to choosing good people', the research says. It found that 'The choice of godparents often honours long friendships, and in choosing them, parents are envisaging a relationship that will last at least 20 years, probably a lifetime.'

One parent I spoke with told me, 'Both times I've found myself looking down at a positive pregnancy test, my first thought was, "Oh God, who's going to help me do this?" Of course I'm lucky in that I have my partner, but in that moment when the reality is beginning to dawn on you, you know you're going to need more than that. It's like that quote from *About a Boy* – two isn't enough. You need backup.'

This desire – for a community of loving adults – has clear implications for mission and ministry, and for what the church can offer to provide what parents want for their children. And it also suggests we would be remiss to overlook the importance of recognizing the godparent/godchild relationship when families come to us for baptisms.

What else do parents value, when it comes to spirituality? The majority of parents with very young children will be under 40. This is relevant, because recent polling for YouGov shows that for the first time, in the last few years, the number of people under 40 identifying themselves as 'nones' – that is, of no religion – passed 50%.

While this may seem like bad news at first glance, this group is not as straightforward as they seem. Linda Woodhead, the author of the research, writes, 'Only a minority of nones ... are convinced atheists ... the largest bloc is made up of maybes, doubters, and don't knows, plus 5.5% who definitely believe in God. As to what kind of God they believe in, less than a quarter of the nones who think there is a God adhere to the traditional idea of a personal "God", with the rest believing in a spirit, life-force, energy, or simply "something there". So the nones are not [a] phalanx of doughty secularists ... but they are certainly more sceptical about the existence of God than those who identify as religious.'

But Woodhead's idea of religion doesn't end with identification – she then goes on to look at practice, where again she finds that 'the picture is not straightforwardly secular ... A quarter [of nones] report taking part in some kind of personal religious or spiritual practice in the course of a month, such as praying. What they absolutely do not do is take part in communal religious practices ... On the whole they do not much care for religious leaders, institutions and authorities, but they tolerate them ... The only leaders for whom nones have regard are Desmond Tutu, the Dalai Lama, and to a lesser extent Pope Francis.[17] It seems clear that nones dislike being preached at and told what to do; they prefer to make up their own minds.'[18]

Woodhead also found that 'nones' are more likely than practising Anglicans to consider themselves global citizens, and in terms of their attitudes towards personal morality, tend to adopt a 'live and let live, as long as you aren't hurting anyone' attitude.[19]

---

17 Interesting question to ponder: what do those three figures have in common? Does your church share those traits?

18 Woodhead, Linda, 'The Rise of "No Religion" in Britain: The Emergence of a New Cultural Majority', *Journal of the British Academy*, 4, 245–61. DOI 10.5871/jba/004.245. Posted 8 December 2016. © The British Academy 2016.

19 For those who like numbers: 83% of Britons fell at the more liberal end of this scale, 92% of lay Anglicans did, and 100% of the 'nones' did.

So families these days form a variety of structures. They may be households consisting of two people or many more. They may have three or more generations living together, may have a single parent or two parents of the same or opposite sex. A child may spend two weekends a month with mum and two with dad, having obvious implications on their participation in weekend activities like Sunday worship. There may be children with additional needs in the family, and both they and their siblings and parents will be affected by this. The family will probably believe in some form of higher power or spirituality, but be suspicious of organized religion and not keen to label themselves as part of a group. They will be likely to have a strong belief in the rights of other families to live as they like as long as nobody is getting hurt, and desire a community of significant adults around them to help raise their children. They value authenticity and community but are sceptical about hierarchy, institutions and authority.

And, crucially, they are unfamiliar with church. Under-40s are less likely to have regularly attended church as a child than any generation of parents before them.

So when you have a family coming for a christening, or to a crib service, or even just an ordinary Sunday morning, you're not just meeting a *child* who isn't enculturated into church, you are likely also encountering *adults* who are unfamiliar with the routines, practices, language, codes of behaviour and general expectations of what going to church means.

This has long-term ramifications in terms of how we help parents to nurture their child's faith at home, when they themselves may be only just starting to explore faith, but it has immediate ramifications in how we welcome these families and treat them on Sunday morning.

I moved house a few years ago, and there was an independent bakery on my new high street. I wanted to go in, but for weeks I put it off and went to the chain one instead. Why? Because I wasn't sure of the rules. Would I have to pay cash, or is card okay? (I don't normally carry much cash.) Do I order and then sit down, or is it table service? I was worried about looking awkward and out of place.

Imagine how much more magnified these emotions must be if the place you're coming to is very quiet and reverent, with a lot of unusual practices like singing together, and you also have a restless two-year-old with you, with an unwieldy pushchair to worry about. Remembering that parents bringing their children to church will probably be uncertain, and nervous about what happens there and what to do, is crucial to creating a culture of welcome.

Many churches now have a page on their church's website about 'What to expect if it's your first time here', as many parents are of the Google generation.[20] 'First impressions are no longer physical but virtual', says the website Church Marketing Sucks.[21] Many parents will have visited your church's website before they come through the doors, and so a culture of welcome may begin online. The Revd Ally Barrett has a guide on how to make a good 'What happens at church' page on your website.[22]

A Church Near You can be a useful resource for those in the Church of England – all churches get a free website and there were 38 million page views on it in 2019. Your diocesan

---

20 You can see one at www.hendonparish.org.uk/worship/what-happens-in-worship/.

21 'How to Welcome People to Your Church'; www.churchmarketing sucks.com/read-this-first/church-visitors/.

22 https://reverendally.org/2018/03/26/first-time-in-church/.

communications team may also have pointers on how to boost your online welcome, or there may be a member of your congregation with digital marketing skills who can donate an afternoon to brush up your online presence.

Simple language, instead of 'church' language, pictures of people instead of an empty church, and a front page with clarity about service times, parking/public transport, accessibility and the church's phone number and email address are the basics for a good website.

Some churches have 'What happens at church' leaflets available at the door. Parents may need to know if there are nappy-changing facilities in the building, and what to do with their pushchair. If Junior Church is available, children might want to meet the leaders before the service starts, and be told that they can stay in church with their parents if they'd prefer. Simply knowing what's happening, and what's expected of you, can go a long way towards making an unfamiliar place feel better. And using ordinary language, not, 'Welcome to the Eucharist; please sit in the north transept by the font' for a first-timer, is also important. If you're feeling especially brave, and open to constructive criticism, why not ask a friend with small children to anonymously visit the church and report back to the PCC or governing body on what the experience was like for them. (You may want to offer free babysitting and/or a pint in return for this.) It can be especially useful if this is a friend who's unfamiliar with church in general.

Again, fish don't know that water is wet – you may not be able to see where your church is failing in welcoming families, but a stranger, with small children, definitely will.

## Discussion Questions

1 When was the last time you went somewhere unfamiliar and new? What emotions did you experience? What helped – or didn't help – you to feel welcome and comfortable? What might your greeting team be able to learn from these experiences?

2 Does the culture of your church value one or two of the types of families above more than the others? How does this preference reveal itself? If you don't know, how could you go about finding out?

3 What messages about families are being sent at services that are more likely to attract children and families, for example Christmas, Mothering Sunday and so on? Which of the family types might feel excluded or invisible in your worship at these times?

4 What challenges and opportunities does this overall profile of the modern family present for your particular context?

# No Time For Sabbath?: Changes in Parents in Work

We've looked at the different types of families that your church may come into contact with, and a bit at how those who aren't affiliated with churches feel about religion and spirituality. But what else is happening in the lives of parents, carers and children that might affect why they come to church and how you can provide a place of welcome to them?

The first major change to have occurred in the past 50 years is the rise in the number of women, including mothers, working outside the home. This has risen steadily since the 1970s.[23] In 2016, over half of households with at least one adult aged 16 to 64 had every member in that age range in employment. Of course, employment may include unsteady or seasonal employment, zero-hours contracts, part-time work or other configurations, but we can safely assume a large number of children are growing up in families where it's normal for all the adults to work.

In lone-parent households, this number is even higher – almost 70% of lone parents are employed.

About a quarter of households with multiple work-age adults have one adult working and one or more not in work, while a little over 10% have no working adults. Some of the households with one parent in work and one not in work will have a parent who stays at home by choice, and are relatively financially secure, while others will have one parent who is unemployed or seeking work and may be in financial need.[24]

One of the most obvious ramifications of this is that for more than half of children, both in two-parent and lone-parent families, family time during the working week will be limited. And for many of these families, this is a struggle. The Modern Families Index suggests that 'a significant proportion of UK's working parents are struggling to cope with the strain of long

23 ONS, 'Women in the Labour Market', 2013; www.ons.gov.uk/ employmentandlabourmarket/peopleinwork/employmentandemployee types/articles/womeninthelabourmarket/2013-09-25.

24 ONS, 'Working and Workless Households in the UK', January to March 2017; www.ons.gov.uk/employmentandlabourmarket/peoplein work/employmentandemployeetypes/bulletins/workingandworkless households/jantomar2017.

work hours – and deliberately stalling and downshifting their careers to reverse the negative impact it is having on family life.'[25] Almost half of parents are putting in extra hours and report that long working hours are affecting their ability to spend time with their family, as well as causing tension at home. Close to 20% have deliberately stalled their careers, refused promotions or switched to part-time work in order to have more time for family life.

So the fact of the matter is that weekends, for parents who work from Monday to Friday, are a time to catch up on what is missed during the week – both in terms of family time and also domestic chores.

So unlike 50 years ago, when it was more likely that one parent would be at home during the week, spending significant amounts of time with young children and looking after the domestic duties, Sunday morning is now a very precious and rare opportunity for families to spend time together.

This may mean that church is less of a priority. The need to get everyone up on time, get dressed and get out the door, after work and school all week (and possibly activities on Saturday), may just be one thing too much. So families who want to come to church, and who might have come every week, might now come once or twice a month, simply because other pressures have increased. And with more people in shift work and the 'gig economy', Sunday may be a workday for at least one parent in more families than in previous decades.

The rise in two-parent working households also means that the church no longer has a large number of skilled, educated

25 www.wordonthestreets.net/Articles/515837/2018_Modern_ Families.aspx.

women available throughout the week to give their time to the church as volunteers – as these women are likely to be in paid employment instead. One of my grandmothers, for example, finished her degree, taught Italian to American GIs during the Second World War, passed the United States Foreign Service Exam, and then quit paid work entirely when she married my grandfather. She was also a skilled seamstress. If a parish could count on three or four such women in the 1970s, giving their time and their skills, it was the equivalent of having a full-time children's worker, administrator and pastoral lay leader. Now, most of those women are using those skills in paid employment, rather than volunteering.

The ripple effect of more women working full time is that older people may be less available in terms of the time they have to volunteer for their church. With childcare prohibitively expensive, many retired people are giving time during the week to care for grandchildren, as both their grandchildren's parents are working.

It may be worthwhile for your church to prayerfully consider how to start making connections with local working families to give them quality time together as a family, or to make childcare easier and more convenient. Free or low-cost breakfast, after-school, or holiday clubs can be a lifesaver for working parents, and give you the opportunity to build relationships with children and their carers. If your church culture is one where dressing in your Sunday best is mandatory and arriving even a minute late gets you 'the look of death', it might be worth thinking about how much effort and commitment it has taken the family to be there at all, and how much it would mean to them for the church to be glad they're there, in all their disorganized glory.

Many churches are finding that this shift is affecting their Sunday schools and Junior churches. As one incumbent in the Church of England says, 'Most of our young families have two working parents, and church is only on the table for them if it can also be family time. They want their kids beside them during worship, not off in a nursery somewhere … [so] we keep Sunday school to two Sundays a month.'

This means that children are present for the entire service the remaining two or three Sundays each month, which implies a certain amount of sound and movement. When people complain, she says, 'When [the complainer is someone] who raised their own kids 40 or 50 years ago, and wants to know why today's kids aren't off somewhere else like theirs were, I find that explaining the big sociological shift to two-income families and those parents' understandable desire to spend time with their kids on the weekends, is sometimes helpful.'

Even with such a large number of children living in households where all the adults work, however, there are still many families with one or more parents at home, and it can be helpful to consider their unique needs as well.

## Martha Was Busy With Many Tasks: Parents at Home

Parents who don't work outside the home fall generally into two categories – those who choose to stay at home, and those are unable to work, or find work.

Most mothers will fall into the former category for at least a few months, while they're on maternity leave, even if they plan to return to work. (While couples have had the option of sharing parental leave more equitably since 2015, research suggests few fathers are taking this up.[26])

Parents who stay at home for years may struggle with social isolation and the sense that they are 'at work' 24/7. They may also feel a sense of crisis as their identity shifts from their professional self to a stay-at-home parent. Obviously, the church has a potential role to play here in providing a community and a space for building friendships, and the possibility for parents to use the skills they developed professionally in the service of either the church itself or local charities known to the church.

If your church has a baby and toddler group, with stay-at-home parents attending, creating connections between this group and the Sunday morning congregation can help bring parents into the wider worshipping community. This means that when children 'age out' of the toddler group, the parent may feel comfortable bringing their child on Sunday morning, because they know the church building and already have a relationship with people who they know will be there. These groups are also opportunities for the clergy to get to know these parents, creating a pastoral relationship that can lead to feeling more welcome on a Sunday morning, and an opportunity to talk about baptism.

But not all parents who stay at home do so voluntarily. Many are unable to find work or unable to work due to disability. This can mean similar feelings of isolation to those who choose to stay at home but also, for many, financial insecurity. The needs of children and families in poverty should be of special concern to a church that follows a God who said 'what you do for the least of these, you do for me.'

---

26  www.bbc.co.uk/news/business-43026312.

# Blessed are the Poor? Families in Poverty

> The family of five share one double bed and one single camp bed. The room also holds all of the family's belongings.

This is not from *Les Miserables* or a Dickens novel. This is Christmas 2017, in the UK.

> There is no communal lounge or kitchen, and just a small toilet with a shower that they share with other families in the block. Amy's brother is disabled and afraid of water, so she helps her Mum wash him in a bucket in the room. Amy and her sister want to be vets when they grow up. But they say they struggle to do the revision they need due to limited space in the room, and limited time after their long journey to and from school.[27]

This is from a report done by Shelter, on the effects on children of living in emergency accommodation. The report states that 128,000 children woke up in temporary accommodation on Christmas Day 2017. Sadly, while many of these families have parents who are out of work, poverty in working families is also on the rise. A report by the Joseph Rowntree Foundation found that 56% of people in poverty were in a household with at least one adult in work. They further found that seven in ten children living in poverty had at least one working parent.[28] So

---

27 Shelter, "'We've Got No Home'": The Experiences of Homeless Children in Emergency Accommodation', 2017; https://england.shelter. org.uk/__data/assets/pdf_file/0008/1471067/2017_Christmas_investi gation_report.pdf.

28  www.jrf.org.uk/report/uk-poverty-2019-20, p. 7.

much of what applies to working parents above also applies to this section.

According to the Children's Society, there are around four million children and young people living in poverty, and almost a quarter of children aged 10–17 living in households with debt have used food banks.[29] Having three or more children, having someone in the family with a disability, being from a BAME (Black and minority ethnic) background or being a lone parent family increases these risks.

This presents a moral challenge to the church's ministry with children in three ways. First, there is the immediate practical problem of responding to child poverty in our own areas. Food banks, breakfast clubs, school holiday meal programmes, after-school clubs with homework help – these are the sorts of ministries your church may already be running, or may be called to begin.

Second, there is the work of advocating for children in poverty in whatever way possible – doing what the Evangelical pastor Jim Wallis calls 'not just pulling people out of the river, but going upstream to see what's pushing them in'.

But the third challenge is the one most relevant to the question of welcome, and that is that the effects of poverty on children are rarely pretty. This has clear ramifications on our ability to welcome children, if we are not prepared to deal with the effect poverty has on them and their behaviour. This was made very

---

29 The Children's Society, 2017, 'Overwhelming Problems Damaging Children's Well-Being: Spotlight on the Impact of Debt and Financial Difficulties on Children'; www.childrenssociety.org.uk/sites/default/files/overwhelming-problems-the-impact-of-debt-and-financial-difficulties-on-children.pdf.

evident in a BBC documentary in 2017, in which the rapper Professor Green returned to the parts of London where he grew up and got to know several families there.

The children he met included:

- A 10-year-old child who self-harms because she doesn't want to show her anxieties to her mother and add to her worries.
- A 12-year-old boy whose mother worries he will be tempted into drug dealing to try and help relieve her money problems.
- A boy who explains how he can't have friends over because he's too ashamed of where he lives.[30]

Living in poverty is living under siege – it is a slow, long-term traumatic event, and depression, stress and anxiety can easily result. And unfortunately, the effects often linger beyond childhood. In a discussion about child poverty on Twitter, a woman who is now financially secure in her thirties described how she still has panic attacks if she can see the backs of her food cupboards.

Children who come to worship with us on Sunday morning, whose lives are full of deprivation, stress and instability, may have significant mental health challenges or behavioural issues. These issues may be obvious – anger, stealing, hoarding – or they may be hidden – self-harm, anxiety.

Of course we need to make sure that all children are safe, and that means not accepting behaviour that is hurtful, even when it comes from a place of hurt itself. But positive behaviour management, based on a foundation of belief that children are *good*, and that we care about them, can make a difference.

---

30  BBC One, 25 September 2017, *Professor Green: Living in Poverty.*

A friend of mine who ministers in a high-deprivation area adds that poverty instils 'a lack of agency'. He recalls a conversation with a 14-year-old in his parish about his lack of homework. 'What's the point?' the child said. My friend says, 'I then had the usual run-down of: no homework results in no qualifications. He said, "So what?" Which results in no job. "So what?" Which results in no money. "So what, no one in my family has a job. I'll just end up on benefits like everyone else." A 14-year-old kid who thought his life was written off before it had even really begun.'

When we welcome children who are living in poverty, we are welcoming 'the least of these', and our call to make church a safe, stable, loving, accepting place for them is a serious and urgent one.

A church that welcomes children can be a place that gives children some of the agency that poverty takes from them. If we can welcome children like the 14-year-old above, we can build trust with them in a way that other places may not be able to. In two years, he will be eligible to join the PCC and help make decisions about his church community. Before then, he can be welcomed, listened to, asked if he'd like to take on a leadership role in worship. God doesn't write anyone off. Neither can we. It is that kind of welcoming love that can change people.

Children who find there is routinely not enough at home can learn that church is a place where there is enough to go around – enough biscuits after the service, enough attention from the adults. They may learn through the rituals and consistency of worship that church is a place where things are stable and reassuring. And they may learn that the love of God is a love that sees past the effects of the trauma they are living with, and loves the child behind the challenging behaviour.

Poverty is often hidden. It may be worthwhile to visit the Church of England stats page at https://www.churchofengland. org/more/policy-and-thinking/research-and-statistics, click on the interactive map, find your parish, and look at the number, ethnic make-up and level of poverty in your parish. A more in-depth look at poverty by parish is provided by the Church Urban Fund, which is also linked from the page above.

## Additional Needs

Over a million children in England are classified as having special educational needs. For some of these children, church is already a more welcoming place than school, because the focus isn't on a particular type of academic achievement but on worship and living in community. However, it's worth looking at what the most common types of special needs are, and how your church may, even unintentionally, be putting up barriers to children and families.

Recently, the needs of those on the autism spectrum have received greater public attention and awareness. Chris Packham's moving BBC documentary about life with Asperger's, Channel 4's *Are You Autistic?* and public awareness campaigns have brought this into mainstream awareness. People on the autism spectrum tend to thrive with predictable routines, an under-standing of what is expected of them (Do I have to put money in the plate? How much?), and there is also a tendency to reach sensory overload very quickly – including not always liking being touched or hugged.

People with autism may develop physical habits to calm themselves when overwhelmed, anxious, or frustrated, called 'stimming' – these might include rocking, flapping and other behaviours. Some people with autism may also approach idiom and metaphor in a literal manner, and have a high recall for details – this can affect how a child understands idiom and metaphor in Scripture or in the language of worship.

Other common additional needs are reading and processing difficulties – if your worship focuses extensively on being able to read long chunks of material, children with dyslexia may struggle. A church whose culture requires being able to sit still and not fidget for an hour at a time may be a challenge for children with attention deficit disorder. Consider what parts of your building are accessible for children who use wheelchairs, and what children's activities they may struggle to fully participate in. Would children with hearing or visual impairments be able to fully participate in your worship?

Also, how would your congregation react to the presence of children whose behaviour may be outside the norm? Would they tut? Scold? Whisper about 'parents these days with no discipline'? Or would they smile, give a helping hand if needed, and let the child and carers take the lead on what the child needs?

It might be worth taking the time to read up on resources led by people and families who have first-hand knowledge of additional needs – the Additional Needs Alliance is a good starting point,[31] as is Amy Fenton Lee's ministry.[32] All Belong has developed resources designed for groups of children with additional needs, especially Down's syndrome.[33] Your church congregation as a whole may benefit from learning more about how children

---

31  http://additionalneedsalliance.org.uk/.
32  https://theinclusivechurch.wordpress.com/.
33  www.allbelong.co.uk/.

with additional needs may react to church, and what can be helpful for them. In specific cases, of course, the parents and the children themselves are the experts – if you already have children in your congregation with additional needs, speak with them and their parents about what church is like for them, and what they need in order to be fully welcomed and included.

And it is important to remember that for many people, their additional needs are not perceived as a disability, but simply a way of being that is different from the majority. The term 'neurodiversity' reflects the fact that this is not a good/better/ best way of being, but simply another way in which humans reflect the diverse faces of God, in how we are made. A culture of welcome is a place where we all appreciate that everyone has something to teach us about who God is. The Body of Christ is richer when people of all ages, and all abilities, are present and are being themselves.

## Discussion Questions

1 What was the most interesting or surprising thing you learned in this chapter?

2 Based on what you've read in this chapter, and your own experiences, what changes might have to happen in your church in order to be welcoming towards children and families?

3 Is there anything you believe you need to learn more about in order to effectively minister to children and families today? Where might you find this information?

4 How can you share what you have learned and discussed with the wider congregation?

# 2

# First Steps and Solid Foundations

Imagine you get invited to a dinner party. You go, and the table is set beautifully, there are candles and lovely table linens, the other guests are dressed impeccably, music plays in the background ... and the other guests and the host couple spend the entire evening bickering and giving each other the silent treatment.

Would you go back?

Or you get invited to a close friend's birthday party. You're looking forward to a relaxing evening sharing what's going on in your lives, having a meal together and meeting some other people who are important to your friend. Then you show up and after a brief obligatory social time, you find that you're actually there because your friend has a new business selling essential oils and she wants you to buy £100 worth and sign up to sell them yourself.

Would you go back?

Because you're amazing and brilliant, you get invited on two dates in the same weekend, both for dinner. On the first one, the minute you arrive, your date asks what your first impressions are. They invite you to their sister's wedding before your starters have arrived. When the bill comes, they ask, 'So, can I change my Facebook status to "in a relationship" yet?' By the time you get home, there are 20 texts from them, asking, 'So how serious are we, really?' and 'Just let me know your ideal partner, and I will totally be them, whatever you want, just tell me.'

The next night, on your other date, this person greets you with a nod. They forget your name three times, and spend most of the dinner checking their phone. All their conversation is talking about themselves, and their achievements. You never hear from them again.

Do you want to go out with either of these people again?

I imagine most people would run screaming from all the above scenarios. Yet they are all ways the church can behave towards new families.

The overly keen date who wants to change his relationship status immediately is the church that invites you on to the coffee rota the second you walk in the door, or asks you to commit your life to Jesus five minutes after you arrive, or is so desperate for young families that they have no identity of their own to offer apart from wanting you there.

The date who spends the evening on his phone is the opposite – the church that is perfectly happy as an exclusive club, and not interested, really, in getting to know new people.

The beautiful dinner party full of arguments is the church torn by factionalism and cliques, while the multi-level marketing scheme is the church that sees you only as a number or a target for their own agenda, not as a person in your own right.

Inviting families to share in the life of the church means inviting them to join a family and be drawn into a relationship. If the family is toxic and dysfunctional, sorting that out is a crucial part of becoming welcoming.

The good news is that there are many ways to be welcoming, not one single right way. But there are a few sure-fire ways to *not* be welcoming. Let's look at a few.

While these case studies are fictional, some of them are based in part on aspects of real situations that I or my colleagues have worked in.

## Case Study One: St Swithun's-in-the-Swamp

St Swithun's is one parish in a largely rural benefice consisting of five churches. There is one incumbent, who works full time. They arrived five years ago, with the understanding that 'reaching out to families' was a priority.

The other four churches have no kitchen or toilet facilities at all – St Swithun's has a port-a-potty and a corner in the back with a kettle and microwave and some storage of cups and plates. There is heating, but it is unreliable.

St Swithun's has received some lottery funding for repairs and renovations, but far short of what is needed. The PCC and the incumbent are working on fundraising and an initial building project planned for next year.

The largely elderly congregation requires significant pastoral care for issues around declining health, loneliness and bereavement, and are increasingly unable to devote time and energy to supporting St Swithun's in its ministry. Some congregation members are still upset about losing a weekly Eucharist when St Swithun's became part of a benefice in the 1990s, and refuse to worship at other churches in the benefice. There is a lot of talk about the 'golden age' when there was a thriving Youth Group and Sunday school at St Swithun's.

A few years ago, when the incumbent was new, they started a Messy Church. This had some initial success, but attendance soon fell off and volunteers left. The incumbent tried to keep it going on their own, but closed it after a year and became very demoralized.

Soon after, they started a baby and toddler group in the village hall – this takes up five hours a week, costs money to hire the hall and often fails to cover its costs, as attendance fluctuates. It also consists mostly of childminders, which means the ability for families to make a connection with the church is limited. The incumbent feels it is an important service to the community, and works hard to keep it going. The PCC questions whether this is the best use of time.

The incumbent also has made six of St Swithun's monthly Eucharists 'All-Age Services' – these are occasionally attended by one or two families, but most of the regular congregation stay away on those days. The PCC has also questioned whether these services are worth continuing.

When the incumbent proposes new ideas for ministry with children, there are questions about resources of time and volunteers, and about whether they would work, since 'Everything else we've tried hasn't done anything'.

The incumbent is frustrated, burned out, and feels like a failure in their ministry.

## Discussion Questions

- Does anything about St Swithun's remind you of your church?

- What needs to happen among the leadership (incumbent and PCC) for them to become a place of welcome towards families?

- What needs to happen among the congregation?

- What would their next steps be?

## Case Study Two: St Cuthbert's in the Car Park

St Cuthbert's is a town centre church, on a rail line to a major city. The area it is in has changed significantly over the last 50 years, becoming more racially and religiously diverse, and with some young families who commute to the major city.

Historically, St Cuthbert's had an Anglo-Catholic tradition, with high-quality choral music, thoughtful preaching and a contemplative atmosphere. Children and young people served as servers and choristers, and there was a large Sunday school, run largely by one member of the congregation. When children were in worship, except when they were serving or singing, they were expected to be 'seen but not heard'. Over the last 50 years, attendance by children and young people has slowly but surely fallen. Many of the current congregation raised their children in this church and remember the days when there were large numbers of children and young people.

The church has a kitchen and a church hall – Sunday school is held in the hall, still run by the same person who has been running it for 25 years. Sunday school largely consists of a story read from a children's Bible, some reading comprehension questions about it, and colouring sheets.

The previous incumbent was at St Cuthbert's for 40 years, and was much loved. The search process for a new incumbent, however, was focused on change and new blood. An incumbent was appointed six months ago – a young married priest with three small children.

Citing much of the same research that was listed in Chapter 1, about the needs of modern families, the new incumbent decided that Sunday school would be limited to one Sunday a month, and the rest of the time, the whole body of Christ would worship together. They announced this decision to the congregation after a month in post.

The person who has led Sunday school for the last 25 years learned of this decision at that service.

The PCC also looked at the times of local sporting events on Sunday mornings, and decided to move the main service time to accommodate them, so families didn't have to choose between sports and church. This was again announced to the congregation once the decision had been made.

A new sub-committee of the PCC has been set up to look at children's ministry, chaired by the incumbent's spouse.

Worship on non-Sunday-school days now includes prayer and discussion stations in place of a sermon, and ten minutes of action songs at the beginning, to encourage children to participate. There is a children's corner at the front of the church, with a ball pit, a train set, a toy kitchen and some puzzles. The priest's three young children often run freely around the church throughout worship, playing with the toys in the children's corner or playing games at the back.

## Discussion Questions

- What has this incumbent done right in their time so far at St Cuthbert's? What have they done wrong?

- In what ways does St Cuthbert's offer a culture of welcome to young children? In what ways does it fail to do so?

- In what ways does St Cuthbert's offer spiritual nurture to children? In what ways does it fail to do so?

- What should the incumbent and the PCC do next?

- Is there anything about St Cuthbert's that reminds you of your church?

## Case Study Three: St Peter's by the Pub

St Peter's is a church in an affluent suburb, with about 200 on the electoral roll. They employ a children's and families worker and an administrator, and have a main Sunday service that has an informal feel to it.

Three years ago, after a period of extended growth among children and families, a parishioner made allegations of abuse against the incumbent. The incumbent had been very active, pastorally, among the young families; many families felt they had a very close relationship, and that relationship was a large part of why they came to St Peter's. The incumbent was suspended and, after an investigation and a trial, convicted and imprisoned. During the time the incumbent was suspended, a number of different clergy covered the services.

The churchwardens, families worker and administrator took on significant extra duties during the suspension and the interregnum. Staff meetings were held on an ad hoc basis, supervision and performance management of staff was suspended, the churchwardens had to deal with an extended legal row over a party-wall agreement on their own and, due to the extra strain on staff and volunteers, small and large mistakes were made. Administrative duties and pastoral care fell through the cracks. Meanwhile, a significant amount of the PCC's time was spent discussing the accusations, and the diocesan and police response to them.

During the course of the investigation, many of the parents openly questioned the truth of the claims against the incumbent, often at church events.

Rumours circulated about who had made the allegations, and what their motives were. Factions began to form between supporters of the incumbent and those who believed the accusations. Comments were made in public about the Christian duty to forgive, and how damaging and disruptive this process was to the whole community.

Those who supported the incumbent were told they were betraying the victim; those who believed the accusations were told they were condemning an innocent person in a personal vendetta, without proof.

Those who believed the accusations felt betrayed and let down by a person they had admired, and this anger was often directed in passive-aggressive ways at the church leadership and other parishioners.

Many families left the church, in many cases feeling bruised by their experiences. Friendships were disrupted. Those who remain members of the church have a survivor mentality, often saying 'If you haven't gone through this with us, you can't understand.'

Now a new incumbent has been installed.

## Discussion Questions

- What, if anything, does St Peter's need to do to get to a place where they can welcome new families?

- If a new family came to St Peter's on a Sunday, what might they experience?

- What different groups and individuals are in pastoral need at St Peter's? What effect does this have on the new incumbent's priorities and time management?

- Does anything at St Peter's remind you of your own church?

I asked a group of clergy, paid lay staff and children's ministry volunteers what the absolute necessities were for a church in terms of groundwork, before they could deliberately move forward in reaching out to and welcoming new families. These are the themes that came up over and over again:

1 A vicar who is not exhausted, cynical or negative. Being cynical and negative are usually by-products of being exhausted. How is the vicar being cared for?

2 Leadership who have the will and, crucially, the *time* to put into this. Simply finding the time may be the work of several years. What can be taken off the vicar's plate? What can be streamlined? Is there anything that can be dropped? Are there volunteers who can be nurtured to take on things the vicar is now doing, freeing the vicar up to lead this process? Do you need an administrator and if so, can you afford one?

3 An attitude of hospitality – things like where to put prams and so on are much easier to deal with if greeters have the right attitude.

4 The right intentions. Jo Wetherall, who is children's ministry advisor in Gloucester, said churches need to 'stop trying to attract families for church growth purposes and concentrate on their spiritual growth'.

5 A willingness of at least a few people to form real relationships with families.

6 A community that knows who they are and are confident – nothing is less attractive than desperation!

In this discussion, one thing that came up over and over again was the attitude of the leadership. A children's worker pointed out that unless clergy are on board, lay leadership will struggle to lead cultural change.

Even if the people in charge of the process are laity – children's and families workers, parents, volunteers – the clergy have a role to play. They must meet regularly with those in charge of the process, find out how things are going, problem-solve together and, crucially, back up the laity when needed. Clergy and leaders who undermine or abandon the lay leadership, while paying lip service to their goals, will doom any process of cultural change.

Of course, this doesn't mean that the clergy have to backup everything the lay leaders do, regardless of whether they agree with it. This is why regular meetings are essential.

Here's an example from my own ministry.

As a new children's worker, I planned an All-Age Christingle service that was a disaster. The reasons why it was a disaster aren't that important – suffice to say, I didn't prepare the worship leaders well, and didn't consider the needs of older worshippers, foolishly assuming that only children and their parents would show up.

My incumbent at the time responded to complaints by saying he fully supported my commitment to creating child-friendly worship, that parts of the service had gone well and that I was new and still learning. He thanked people for their feedback and assured them I would learn from it. Then he met with me and helped me deal with the embarrassment I felt, and plan how to do better next time.

Clergy can also set and enforce the message that becoming more welcoming to children and families isn't a zero-sum game. It doesn't mean choosing between the needs of children and the needs of older people. As Nicola Bown, an Anglican curate said, churches need to do 'a serious consideration of how to welcome both families and old people in the same space. How do we welcome people with mobility needs and deafness *and* provide a play space and welcome children's noise? How do we show that we value children *and* old people – both are vulnerable groups? It's often said that children are the church's present as well as its future; but that is also true of old people. In an ageing population old people must be part of the church's future.'

Others in the discussion that led to this list agreed. Older people carry the history of the church community, and probably many decades' experience of following Jesus, and can pass that wisdom, experience and collective memory on to future generations. They can form (safe) friendships with younger families and create that village we talked about in Chapter 1. Intergenerational community is also an important way for children to learn about the needs of others – 'Be careful for toddlers and people with sticks!' is something I often say to the older children at my church. After all, what better place is there than church for a child to learn how to love, and look out for, a neighbour who has different needs?

So clergy can make things harder for themselves by setting up the process as antagonistic from the start – 'We are choosing children over you; get on board or get out'. Instead, the message can be, 'We are choosing to be generous and to share what we love about God and this church with children and those who care for them, and to have our own faith renewed by learning from them as well.'

## Knocking Down Barriers

In addition to leadership and management issues, there can be other barriers to families. Some of these are relatively easy to remove, some may take longer. But removing them is an important first step towards changing the culture and becoming more welcoming to families.

You may feel tempted to start up something else to make contact with families immediately, while you work on removing bigger barriers. This may be the right thing, but I encourage you to think it through carefully. Removing barriers to welcome is often a team effort. And it takes time. So it may be too much to ask, at the start, that a church starts up programmes outside Sunday morning, *and* works on changing the Sunday-morning culture.

For example, you may need to make changes to your building – like adding a loo – to make it more possible for families to be included in worship. So if there's only one member of clergy and no paid staff, it's a lot to expect the church to keep doing everything they're already doing, manage the building project and, at the same time, start up a Messy Church in the village hall.

Archdeacons, bishops, diocesan staff and others who have an eye on Statistics for Mission and other measures of growth, especially around children's ministry, need to keep this in mind. As I often say to churches, 'If your children's work for the next five years is to build a toilet with nappy-changing facilities and a kitchen, and you don't see a single child for those five years, then that's your children's work.'

Of course, theoretically that church could be doing Prayer Spaces in Schools, assemblies, Messy Church in other locations, and myriad other types of children's ministry while they wait for the building project to be done. However, unless those things are *already in place*, asking a church to start them up while simultaneously laying the groundwork for cultural change in the traditional model of church may be impossible, unless the church is large, wealthy and has a significant number of paid staff. Clergy burnout and the volunteer crisis are real challenges.

Some of the barriers may lie in the areas of problems with buildings, and volunteers and expertise.

### Problems with the building

A building without toilets or a kitchen can be a difficult place for families, especially those with under-5s. A building without working heating, or with a leaky roof, or with no place for children to move around, or for prams (possibly with sleeping occupants) or scooters to be stored safely, is a church that will struggle to be welcoming to children and families.

Kathleen, whose daughter is almost four, says, 'When my daughter was still in nappies, we didn't go anywhere that didn't have a nappy-changing surface of some kind. If I had to kneel on the floor to change her once, we never went back to that place. [And] during the year in which she has become accustomed to toilets, I didn't go anywhere that didn't have toilets, because it led to a huge scene. She wouldn't go outside, she would try to hold it, then she'd have an accident and flip out … In the first three to four years of life, I'd say … prioritizing toilets is a huge way to remove barriers for families to attend.'

To see how widespread this attitude was, I did a Twitter poll – not the most scientific of methods, I admit, but often a good snapshot. Out of almost 100 parents who responded, 84% said they wouldn't consider going back with their child to a place that didn't have toilets.

If you can't install a toilet, or don't want to wait years and spend tons of money doing so, is there a building close to the church that would let you use their toilets for Sunday morning and during any toddler groups? The vicarage? A pub? The school? How can you let parents know this is available?

We'll look more into the question of how to get 'quick wins' with your building in the next chapter.

## Volunteers and expertise

Some churches have children in main worship, for the whole service every week, but most churches will still want to do some form of Junior Church. Even those who want to include children in worship for the whole service, and do away with Junior Church entirely, may need volunteers who know about children's spirituality to help with worship planning. Or there may be several people who are willing to help with this work, but aren't sure of their skills. Identifying possible volunteers, and ensuring they and the leadership have access to the right kind of training and support, may be a process that takes several years.

Research has found that the decline in volunteer numbers among the church is real and shows no signs of stopping. Dr Abby Day, the author of *The Religious Lives of Older Laywomen*, says, 'While elderly laywomen have never been given a formal voice or fully acknowledged by the Church, they are the heart, soul and driving organizational force in parishes everywhere. Their loss will be catastrophic.'[34]

The generation currently in their 70s and 80s have spent their lives volunteering for the church, but according to Dr Day, 'their willingness to work without reward for the Church has not been found among their children or grandchildren'.[35] Younger people, she says, even those of faith, tend to volunteer through activism or other ways in the community, rather than through church.

The structures of the Church of England have not caught up with this reality. While some churches are fortunate enough to be able to employ administrators, children's and families workers, youth workers and more, many are still trying to do everything those larger churches do, with only a vicar and volunteers (or not even a vicar – many rural churches are effectively lay led, being in vacancy for years at a time, or sharing one member of clergy between five or six parishes).

With some forward-thinking and notable exceptions, few central diocesan or national funds exist to help churches pay

---

34 Day, Abby, quoted in http://blackchristiannews.com/2017/04/church-of-england-facing-a-crisis-because-generation-of-older-women-helpers-are-dying-out/.
35 Ibid.

for extra members of staff, to provide ongoing work at a parish level in children and young people, or take the administrative burden off the clergy and liberate them to start this work. As one Anglican curate says, 'With multi-parish benefices, and dwindling numbers of clergy, it seems that parish clergy are just fire-fighting all the occasional offices and regular Sunday worship commitments to keep the ship afloat.'

The assumption, looking at the structures, is that we are still living in the world of James Runcie's Grantchester novels – a paid incumbent, supported by a stay-at-home partner to be his social secretary and hospitality manager, backed up by a village full of women who are home during the day and have plenty of time to clean the vicar's house for him, cook his meals, deal with his correspondence, bring pastoral concerns to his attention, clean the church, visit the sick, look after the garden and churchyard, iron the linens, polish the brass, plan and lead Sunday school, and so on ... The Church of England survived for generations on the unpaid labour of women. This is no longer feasible.

So given this change, it may be that you need to spend some time in discernment, taking stock of what your church has available in terms of time, treasure and talents. There is an audit below that can help you look at this, and you may be surprised by how much you actually have to work with. From there, with a realistic picture of what you have, you can then decide how best to move forward sustainably.

Perhaps, before you can create a culture of welcome for children and families, you need to create a culture of ownership, embedding stewardship and volunteering as an ethos in your church, so that your church understands that ministering to each other, and to newcomers, is the ministry of all the baptized. This may take a while in and of itself. Trying to skip this step, and move straight to growth and welcome for families without changing the expectation that one person will do everything, is a recipe for burnout.

Or you may simply not have much of a pool of potential volunteers. Your congregation may consist largely of people who are infirm or very time-poor. In this case, you may need to embark on a congregational journey of discernment to determine if there's anything you're doing now that can be scaled back or eliminated in order to make it possible for the clergy or PCC to focus on children and families. This needs to be done with great sensitivity and with open-mindedness – that coffee morning for the elderly, attended by only three people each week, which the PCC sees as a waste of time, may be the only opportunity those three people have to leave their houses and socialize each week, and may in fact be a vital fight against loneliness and isolation.

Or perhaps you may decide to do things in a way that doesn't require constant, week-in-week-out commitment from volunteers – for example, instead of Junior Church, make your worship more accessible to children and newcomers, and then use volunteers a few times a year to do special events like pancake parties, holiday clubs and so on. People may be more willing to do a time-limited one-off than a regular ongoing commitment.

One part of this process is considering how what is already existing could be *transformed*. This may lead you to an unexpected place. You might have picked up this book assuming you would end up working on becoming more welcoming on Sunday mornings, and find that this process of discernment leads you to begin a mid-week ministry. Departing from the journey you expected can be a good thing.

For example, you may find that the mid-week coffee morning for the elderly can turn into an intergenerational baby and toddler group, where the current attendees can socialize with each other and *also* form relationships with young parents and children, finishing with a Bible story and some prayers. Suddenly, instead of eliminating this programme, you have kept what mattered to those attendees – time to get out and socialize – and begun a mid-week intergenerational worship community at the same time. Think creatively. Listen with pastoral sensitivity. Instead of thinking, 'I just have to work myself, and the few volunteers we have, harder, and do more', think, 'What could we do differently? And what could we let go, to liberate ourselves to do something else instead?'

If it does come to having to eliminate valuable work that is already happening, make sure that this decision is done communally, not by the incumbent swooping in and shutting something down that has been built, nurtured and valued.

Boundaries are also crucial. If you have slowly lost volunteers over the years, and the few remaining ones, plus the clergy, have picked up everything that used to be done by 20 people, it won't be feasible to transform your welcome to children and families without letting *something* go.

Present this conundrum to the congregation at large – 'We need to do more. We can't do more with what we have. What are our choices?' You may find that a donor miraculously pops up with money to hire an administrator part-time, freeing up the clergy (miracles do happen, allegedly …). Or you may find that one or two new people do volunteer for things.

But you may find that neither of these things happen, and you have to make choices to let things go. In this case, the congregation has been forewarned and given every opportunity to make their voices heard and offer their time or money to help prevent this situation. You have made it clear that the leadership (stipendiary and voluntary) cannot do everything. If this means some things don't get done, that's simply the natural consequences of the situation. Sometimes seeing natural consequences in action is what spurs people to take responsibility.

## Case Study

For three years the curate ran monthly Youth Group sessions on a Friday evening. When the curate left, the congregation assumed the vicar would take these over.

The vicar repeatedly told the congregation that Friday was their day off and they would not be able to lead these sessions. They made announcements in church asking for volunteers and offering to meet with and train anyone who was willing to lead these sessions. They repeatedly emailed the PCC and asked for volunteers, or suggestions for people to approach. Parents of regular Youth Group attendees were asked.

Nothing happened. The prevailing assumption was that if nobody else came forward, the vicar would sigh, go 'Oh, I suppose I'll do it then', and take on this additional responsibility (sacrificing part of their day off), plus the planning and administrative work of the Youth Group.

The day of the first scheduled meeting approached and there was still nobody willing to take it on. The vicar sent out an email and put a sign up on the church saying that Youth Group was cancelled indefinitely due to lack of volunteers.

There was predictable outrage from the congregation. How dare there not be Youth Group! Didn't the vicar understand how crucial Youth Group was to the church's ministry and mission? Weren't young people important? The vicar agreed, but stated again that this was something they couldn't do.

Eventually, two people from the PCC volunteered to lead the Youth Group. They changed its format and structure significantly. The vicar told me, laughing, 'I'm desperate to go in there and make them do it *my* way, the way my curate and I came up with!' But having put so much work into creating that boundary, they knew that handing over control meant handing over control.

Similarly, I once worked with a volunteer team that had dwindled to two elderly women who were doing Messy Church entirely on their own.

'How can we make people see how tired and burned out we are, and come help us?' they asked. 'We can't keep doing it by ourselves for ever.'

'Then why,' I asked, 'are you, in practice, continuing to do it by yourselves for ever?'

I suggested that as long as people knew they would rush in at the last minute and save Messy Church, there was no incentive for anyone else to help them. Maybe seeing something begin to fail is the push the congregation need to take responsibility for it, or else decide, through their inaction, that it didn't matter enough to them to save it.

The congregation's actions, in the face of a failing Messy Church, would then give the two volunteers a choice – did it matter enough to the two of them to keep spending their energy on it, knowing the congregation wasn't going to help them? If so, they would then need to own that choice, knowing it was, in fact, one they had made, not something beyond their control that had been foisted on them. Owning our choices is empowering – even though the actions may look the same as before. Knowing that this is a choice we're making, and that there are other choices, helps us feel more in control of what we do.

If you're going to change to become more welcoming to children and families, other things may need to be dropped. A church with dwindling volunteer numbers and overstretched leaders can't do everything. Sometimes drawing a clear boundary is the way to make a congregation realize that leaders don't have infinite time, choices need to be made, and that if something matters to them, *they* need to take responsibility for it. If they step up, great. If not, then that shows you what choice they've made and puts the ball back in your court. Boundaries and choices, and the realization that you can't change other people but you can change how you respond to them, are crucial before embarking on any deliberate process of change.

## The Parable of the Talents

Another big mistake that many church leaders make is to underestimate how many resources you already have. Many church leaders look around a church with an ageing congregation, no dedicated children's space and few children attending on Sunday morning, and think that they have to start from scratch. But most churches, when you actually take stock of what you have, have the beginnings of what you need already in place.

This is because children's ministry in every church will look different. It will reflect who you are and what your community and worship are like. You don't need to find the clone of that children's worker in that other church down the road and model your building exactly on theirs, and get the same expensive resources they have. You'll do it your way.

Also, don't worry if you haven't got 20-somethings and 30-somethings to lead your children's or youth ministry. You don't need them. Remember, authenticity is what matters. As Peter Landry wrote in the *Church Times*, 'There is a misconception that young people are like magpies, attracted by sparkly things. You don't need to have a high-tech, polished church service in order to attract young people. You don't need to … have hip-hop worship.'[36]

Authenticity and community can be provided by people of any age and background, as long as they genuinely and sincerely care about children, families and young people. When I was a teenager, the person at church, apart from my parents, who I was closest to was an elderly woman with a bad hip and several cats – I visited her apartment and we watched film musicals together and she fed me and asked about my life. When she died, her funeral was full of children and teenagers from our church. And a friend of mine fondly recalls the group of 80-something women in her tiny rural parish church who 'loved her into faith' as a teenager. Landry goes on to say, 'In a world that values sparkle over substance, young people are far more attracted to

---

36 Though if this is what's right for your context and community, go for it.

a church where they are welcomed, genuinely loved, seen as equals, valued as individuals, invested in, and given the tools to live as Christians within their lives outside of the church.'

Undervaluing what you already have can mean you miss opportunities and make things harder than they have to be.

It might help to do this audit as a group, or to do it individually and then share your thoughts. The group might be the PCC, a working group or something else. But this is not an exercise for one person to do on their own. You may want to do it with the whole congregation together – if not, think about how the group will share their thoughts with the rest of the congregation and get their input. If you have children and young people in your congregation, even one or two, can they be included in these discussions?

The audit is broken down into the three Ts of stewardship – time, talent and treasure. These are the things we have to give to God and to each other. Those who may not have much of one may have some of one of the others to give.

Please note: you do not have to answer yes to *all* these questions in order to get started! This is not a test – it's an evaluation tool to see where you are, what gifts your congregation has, and to help you think about how to proceed. If you answer yes to even one question, that tells you something about what you can do and where you can go.

Also note that when the audit refers to 'people', this doesn't just mean 'adults'. The person skilled in hospitality may be 10 or 100.

# RESOURCE AUDIT – what do we already have?

## *Time*

What are the total number of clergy and staff hours available to this church during a typical week? What are they spent on?

What support is given during a typical week by volunteers? What tasks are done?

Is there anything that is taking up a disproportionate amount of time, by clergy and staff or by volunteers? What can be done about this?

Are there any potential volunteers who might have some time to give on a regular basis?

Are there any potential volunteers who might have some time to give on an occasional/seasonal basis?

Are there any tasks (especially administrative) that could be done by volunteers at home?

What time is spent during the week, by members of the congregation, either being with children or working on their behalf? Is that being noticed and celebrated?

How much time during the week is the church open for prayer?

How much time during the week is the church used by community groups? Do any of these groups include children or families?

## *Talents*

Who among your congregation has skills in helping or therapeutic work? (Current or retired teachers, therapists, counsellors, social workers, health visitors, midwives, doctors and so on.)

Who among your congregation has a calming and loving presence, who might be able to be on 'cuddle duty' to help with babies? (This could be a teenager, a 90-year-old or anybody in between.)

If you don't have an administrator, are there people in your congregation with administrative/organizational skills?

Who if anyone among your congregation is skilled in social media and/or marketing?

Is there anyone in your congregation with fundraising experience?

Is there anyone in your congregation with special skills that could be used with children on Sunday morning, either in worship or Junior Church – painting, woodworking, music, drama and so on?

Are there people in your congregation skilled at hospitality? For example, baking, chatting to strangers?

Are there people who would be comfortable building community connections with shops, children's services for example. – to help raise the church's profile in the local area, publicize what you're doing and so on?

Is there someone who has the writing skills to do warm, personal baptism anniversary cards, invitations to events, for example?

Do you have knitters, sewers or other crafty people who could make resources or baptism gifts?

Who in your congregation encounters God closely through prayer? Could they be asked to pray for children and families in your community?

Is there anyone in your congregation skilled at working with space – setting up spiritual play spaces, displays, Easter gardens and so on?

Are there any other talents that might be useful for ministering with children and families?

Based on this list, what unique gifts does your church have to offer children and families in your community?

## *Treasure*

What are the church's main sources of income?

Does the church talk regularly about stewardship? Legacies?

Are there people with the means to support children's ministry resources or training, who might be approached for specific donations?

Is there a way of using the church space to generate more income, and are there people who can take on the administration of that?

Do you have community links with businesses who might be interested in sponsoring activities for children and families?

Does your diocese have resources on stewardship, or a stewardship officer, who might help you find ways to increase your income?[37]

## Discussion Questions

1 What work needs to be done in preparing the ground? Who can do this work?

2 What do you value about your church community? How visible are these things to new people on a Sunday morning?

3 How are you feeling about the process at the moment? Excited? Intimidated? Worried? All of the above?

4 Are there lingering issues from the past that are preventing your congregation from being able to be welcoming to new people? How can you address and heal these well? Who can help you do this?

5 Does something else need to be let go, in order to free up time, energy and enthusiasm for children's ministry? What is the process of doing that well?

---

37 All Churches Trust now gives grants specifically for work with children – more information is at www.allchurches.co.uk/growinglives. There are more funding opportunities listed on the CTBI page at https://ctbi.org.uk/funding-links/.

# 3

# The Building, or Who Fits in the Boat?

I remember standing in the line to go up for communion at the church where I was the children's worker, with Olivia, then about ten years old. Our church has exposed rafters with painted designs, and she was admiring them.

'Imagine the church is flipped upside-down', I whispered. 'And that's the bottom. It would be like a really big boat.'

'Like Noah's Ark', she said.

A few years earlier, I'd been exploring the Noah story with a group of children and pre-teens, and asked them what they thought the most important part of the story was. April, then 12, fidgeted with the sleeve of her hoodie and said, 'I think the most important part is that Noah made a big boat, with room for all the animals. He knew the flood was coming – he could have made a small boat, and still saved himself and his family. But he made a big boat with room for everyone.'

Over and over, in the Bible, God's people are challenged to make their boats bigger and let more people in. Our church buildings can and should be like the ark – a place of refuge from the storms of the world outside, a place not just for Noah and his family (the insiders), but metaphorically 'big' enough to be 'a big boat with room for everyone'.

Your building may have massive structural issues that get in the way of welcoming children and families. There may be no toilets or kitchen. You may not be wheelchair/pram accessible. You may be trying to decide if, or how, to remove pews. But just because there are big issues that need time and money to truly solve, that doesn't mean there aren't quick wins you can manage fairly easily.

If you have someone whose knees can take it, I suggest going around your church on your knees to make yourself a child's height. This perspective – What can you see? What's too high for you to reach? – can be useful in helping you think about your space.

You could also give children video cameras (or ask their parents to let them use their phones if they don't have their own yet) and have them record what they see; a few churches in the Diocese of Aberdeen and Orkney did this during worship, and the results are illuminating.[38] What can you see during worship? A lot of the backs of strangers' heads. A lot of bums as people walk in. What can't you see? The altar. Flowers. Icons. Carvings. Stained glass. And you can't hear anything. Of course you're bored.

If you have a community space or church hall, can the children see the displays? Are any of the displays about or for them, or is it all geared towards adults? Are any things they made ever used in worship? I've made bread, stoles, decorated candles, paper

38 You can see the child's-eye-view in a three-minute compilation video at https://aoepiscopal.scot/mission-ministry/children-families/visiting-church-child/.

altar frontals, cloth banners and more with children, all of which were then included – either temporarily or permanently – in the main worship space. This makes the space look like a place where children are included (a visual signal for new-comers) and, for the children who made these elements, tells them that they are part of the community and their offerings are important to the whole community.

What you do with your space can help shift the church com-munity's culture as well. Dean Pusey, a former diocesan youth officer, worked with a church whose churchyard was used as a cut-through by many of the local secondary-school pupils coming to and from school. The PCC decided to use this foot traffic to start making contact – they set up 'Choc Stop', a free hot chocolate stand in the churchyard for six Wednesdays in the winter term, at home time. The vicar was on hand to serve chocolate, the church was open, and volunteers (DBS-checked) were present to talk and, if they wanted, pray with the young people either in the churchyard or inside the church.

After the trial six-week period, I asked Dean what difference he thought it had made. Of course, there were numbers to quote about how many young people the church had made contact with, and the fact that they had been encouraged to enter the church and feel they had a right to be there – but there was also another change he had noticed. 'This church', he said, 'now sees itself as a church that does youth work. They think of them-selves differently.'

Small changes to your space can help your church start to see itself as 'a church that does children's ministry', and this shift in perception is an enormous part of changing a culture. If you have ministry with children outside Sunday morning, make sure that it is featured somewhere in the church building – a display, or examples of the work done there. Reminding the Sunday congregation of the existence of your toddler group, or your Messy Church, or your school assemblies, or the Scout group that meets in your building, and including those groups in your Sunday morning prayers, builds the connection between these ministries and your Sunday congregation, and helps your Sunday congregation see their church as one that does ministry with children. Thinking of yourself as 'a church that does children's ministry' means it's less of a shock when a family actually turns up on Sunday morning. (And seeing a big toddler group display will also send a visual signal to that family that they're welcome here.)

If you have nothing like this, but you do even a few baptisms every year, you could (with permission from parents and carers) display the names and dates of upcoming and recent baptisms, and put up photos from the services if they take place outside the main Sunday service. Include the names of children being baptized in your prayers.[39]

When I asked parents and church leaders about other quick wins that could be done to make the building better, they were relentlessly focused on the practical. One mum said she wanted 'a First Aid box where you can find it, and boxes of tissues to hand'. Other parents suggested a sign to make it clear where your buggy can go, so you don't feel like 'the stupid new person who doesn't know how things work here' the second you walk in. One dad, who's sick of changing nappies on the floor, said that if you have a toilet with a nappy-changing table, it should either be a unisex toilet or there should be one in the

---

39 For more on connecting baptism ministry with the ongoing life of the church, see *Life Events: Mission and Ministry at Baptisms, Weddings, and Funerals*, by the Revd Dr Sandra Millar, and the articles and ideas at https://churchsupporthub.org/baptisms/.

gents as well. They also want juice and unbreakable cups available after church, along with the tea and coffee for the adults. Sarah Moore, a URC minister, said churches would ideally have 'somewhere that isn't the toilet for mums to breastfeed. And an attitude of toleration towards breastfeeding.'

When I was a children's worker, I added myself to the greeting team at the door every week, to be on hand specifically to welcome children and their carers. I made sure to get down to their level, greet them by name if I knew them, introduce myself if I didn't, and point out to new children and their adults what their choices were – that Sunday school was available but not mandatory, that we had a children's area if they needed it, and where the toilets were. Do you have one or two people who can take on this role (maybe even children or teenagers themselves)? Or could you help your existing greeters do this?

But one of the most transformative quick wins, from a spirituality point of view, is to use your space to help children engage more fully in worship.

## Beyond the Children's Corner: It Starts With a Better Children's Corner

Don't skip this section if you think you have no room for a children's corner. I'm just saying that now before your eyes glaze over. Hang on – because there are ways of doing something even in the most rigid church with no space.

I think we're all familiar with the cycle. A young family comes to church and sits at the back. The rest of the congregation look at them the way most people would look at a ticking suitcase with wires coming out of it. The parents have that hollow-eyed hunted look of panic, or else a defensive and combative 'I dare you to say something' expression.

Sure enough, ten minutes into the service, the two-year-old starts whining. The parents frantically shush them and shove raisins in their face, or else they ignore them. The kid gets more bored, and the behaviour escalates. Before you know it, the child is having a full-scale meltdown, the parents are taking the kid out of the service (or else sitting there while the tantrum takes over worship), and the rest of the congregation is annoyed, because the service turned into the sideshow to a miserable two-year-old.

The family never comes back.

The congregation becomes more entrenched in their conviction that children disturb the service and parents these days have no discipline.

And the child learns that church is a boring place with nothing to offer them – not a place where their spirituality is nurtured, accepted and given space.

Many churches have picked up on this cycle, and have provided a children's corner as a way of breaking it. Some of these, I hate to say, are among the most depressing places in existence. Here are a few real-life examples:

• The children's corner is in the church porch outside the north chapel. There is no heat. You can see through glass doors into the church itself.

- The children's corner is at the back of the church. All you can see from there is the back of the last row of pews. It is furnished with Thomas the Tank Engine toys with pieces missing, and a few stuffed toys that haven't been washed since at least the 1980s. There is a table with colouring sheets of flowers and Peppa Pig, and a plastic basket with a few broken crayons in it.
- The children's corner is also the church office, walled off at the back of the church with glass. There is no audio projection of the service into this space. You are surrounded by bookshelves, a desk and filing cabinets. Through the glass at the front of this space, you can kind of see a few of the pews.

Writing about these kinds of spaces, Rebecca Nye says, 'This all conveys a careless mindset, a "none of this really matters" attitude, a message about being second-rate. It sends a negative message about how children are valued by God and in this place.'[40] The Revd Dr Sandra Millar bluntly calls them 'dead teddy graveyards'.

But children's corners in churches can, if done with care and consideration, be places that nurture spirituality and engage children in worship. (Many of these principles also apply to spaces where Junior Church and other activities take place.)

The key is to start thinking of them not as places to distract children but as places to help children worship. And one of the ways children worship is through play.

Imaginative spiritual play is how young children engage with and make meaning of the stories, liturgies and seasons of our

---

40 Nye, Rebecca, *Children's Spirituality: What it is and Why it Matters*, London: Church House Publishing, 2009, p. 43.

faith. Very young children will copy what they see – a viral video from 2014 showed a toddler, whose parent is a choir conductor, perfectly mimicking the movements and expressions of conducting.[41] In a less sublime example, a friend's daughter, at age three, got into her toy car and immediately started swearing and making rude gestures at imaginary other drivers (because that's what Mummy did! And Mummy realized she needed to adapt her behaviour around her daughter as a result of this episode …).

Copying adults through play is one way young children make sense of the world, try on different roles within it and gain a sense of agency and mastery over the situations of their lives. Having a toy altar (even just a plastic IKEA table with a cloth over it), with a cup and a plate, some toy bread with Velcro so it can be 'broken', some LED candles, a cross and some plastic flowers can help children 'play church' in worship, copying what they see happening up front and integrating this scenario as part of who they are and what their lives consist of. A doll in a christening gown, with a shell, a candle and a wooden dove, can help children who are visiting with a baptism family, or these could even be taken home with older siblings ahead of a baptism.

Both the examples above relate to liturgy. You can also have materials within your children's corner that relate to Bible stories and to the seasons of the church year.

A box or bag containing a toy shepherd and sheep set, a play-mat, some wooden fences and trees, and a storybook of the Lost Sheep and a book of Psalm 23 can introduce children to this

---

41 It's worth a look if you haven't seen it, at www.youtube.com/watch?v=gE9r1LkRCV0.

*The Pray and Play corner in the south aisle of St George's, Campden Hill. Note child-sized altar, sightline to the front, and a variety of themed baskets, as well as meditative colouring of lines from the Psalms, for older children.*

powerful imagery and the stories related to it. A Nativity set or Noah's Ark are easy to find second-hand in charity shops and can start your imaginative spiritual play collection. I've included a list at the end of the book of some of the boxes I've put together over the years, and what they contain – including Pentecost, Creation/Harvest and Easter. The ones related to seasons can rotate, or they can stay out all year, allowing children to use whatever they're interested in.

Having items related to Bible stories helps your space be welcoming to older children as well – once they've moved on from directly copying adults, and are capable of following a more complex narrative, children become much more invested in stories, playing with them to decide what they mean and identifying with their characters.

Betty Pedley, a former children's work advisor, suggests the use of Liturgy Boxes, which parents and small children can use together, either in a children's corner or in the pew. They contain items such as: linking toys for the gathering part of the worship, a laminated card with 'Sorry' on one side (with a picture) and 'Forgiven!' on the other (with a picture) to be used at the confession, a sheep toy for the Agnus Dei and more. You can learn more about Liturgy Boxes at the Spiritual Child Network.[42]

Apart from themed bags or boxes, the following materials can help facilitate imaginative spiritual play:

- Puzzles showing Bible story scenes;
- Books of Bible stories, or prayers, or about worship (SPCK's *Pray, Sing, Worship* is a good guide to the communion service);
- Word searches (you can make your own online);
- Crossword puzzles;
- Dress-up costumes (both 'Bible times' and vestments);
- Mini versions of church stuff;
- Toy churches/Bible story sets – Playmobil has a toy 'wedding' church, as well as Roman and Egyptian items for stories. Be

---

42 http://www.spiritualchild.co.uk/liturgyboxes.html.

aware of small pieces in Playmobil around children under three;

- Colouring for meditation (Often, occupying our hands settles our brain and helps us pay attention better. This is visible in every meeting where adults pretend to take notes but instead are doodling. Some churches now have knitting available for adults to take during the service, adding rows to scarves that will then be donated to a homeless shelter. It's also why I play Bejeweled, or quilt, while watching TV, and why some schools give kids fidget toys during class discussions);
- A prayer wall, prayer tree, and so on;
- Storytelling materials, such as Godly Play boxes;
- Knitted Nativities/Noah's Arks and so on, especially if hand-made by members of your congregation.

The purpose of this space is not to entertain, or educate, but to facilitate worship. It is not intended to 'occupy the children' but to help them engage with church. I've found it useful to refer to them not just as 'Children's Corners' but as 'Pray and Play areas', to make their purpose clear. (One church I know calls theirs The Prayground.) Your Pray and Play area may be used for the whole service or for the start and end times, if you have Junior Church – having a space like this to come back to, after a Junior Church session where toddlers may be encouraged to move and jump and play, can help ease the transition back into the main worship service. It may be there all the time or only come out when you have All-Age Worship.

Many of these items can be collected over time, from charity shops, nearly-new sales and so on. Others can be made. Your diocese may have items you can borrow, so you can rotate what you have available throughout the year for no cost. A Pray and Play area with a good variety of items can be put together for £200 to £300, or less if you have mostly hand-made or second-hand items – and certainly no more than £500, even if you buy many things all at once and all brand new. You can start simple and add to it over the years, as and when funds become available.

Here are some things to think about if you're considering setting one up:[43]

- Where will you put it?
  - Can children see what's happening at the front of the church?
  - Is it warm enough? Or, at least, not any colder than the rest of the church?
  - Can latecomers sneak in easily without feeling conspicuous?
  - Can a child who needs a nappy change/some time away/ breastfeeding be removed easily?
  - Does it feel part of and connected to the main worship area?
  - What can be heard, smelled, touched?
- Who will it be used by? Babies and toddlers only, or older children as well? What about children visiting for baptisms, weddings or funerals?
- Have you considered health and safety – avoiding toys with small pieces, having a soft floor covering, minding sharp corners at toddler head height, having coverings for electrical sockets? (A soft floor covering also reduces the effect of a three-year-old banging the tiger from the Noah's Ark on the floor in your echoing building.)

---

43 Many of these questions are included in the Diocesan *Pray and Play* leaflet, which my predecessor at St Albans, the Revd Ruth Pyke, originally put together.

- Have you made sure, for the well-being of sleep-deprived parents and everyone else, that any toys that make a noise have had their batteries removed?
- Are there adult-sized chairs or benches, so parents and carers can stay with their children? This isn't a crèche.
- How will you keep it tidy? One church I know has a coloured sticker on each of their themed boxes, and every item has a matching coloured sticker, so parents and children can easily tell where everything goes. But things will still get put back wrong, mysterious items like toy cars will appear out of nowhere, and so on. Who will check in once a month or so to make sure all is as it should be?

If you don't have the space for a Pray and Play area, many of these same principles can be applied to what goes on in the pews. You can have bags available at the entrance to the church, containing toys, Bible/worship books, colouring sheets and crayons, puzzles and so on, which children can use in the pews. Parents and carers can be encouraged to sit somewhere where their child can see something other than the back of a stranger's head, but where they can still escape easily for nappy changes and meltdowns, for example.

With a Pray and Play area, or pew bags, when a child starts to fidget or move around in worship, instead of the parents shushing them while the congregation glares, the parents can provide a place where the child can engage imaginatively with the stories, symbols and images of Christian faith.

So instead of *the family never comes back*, you have a family who knows there is a place for them in church, and they feel more relaxed and confident about coming.

Instead of *the congregation becoming more entrenched in their conviction that children disturb the service and parents these days have no discipline*, you have a congregation gradually realizing that tantrums aren't inevitable, and if the children have something to engage them, the more peaceful parts of the service are less likely to be full of piercing screams. They therefore become less hostile and defensive towards new families, and less critical towards parents and carers.

And instead of *the child learns that church is a boring place with nothing to offer them*, that child learns that church is a place where you can play and move around (even a little bit, kneeling backwards in a pew to set up a Nativity set on the seat, for example), and still be in worship – a place where you hear music and stories, where you pray, a place that may have beautiful candles or windows or flowers to look at, a place where you can explore, encounter awe and wonder, and be welcomed and included as you are.

The Revd Lucy Davis, a parish priest in a small town in Bedfordshire, says that 'creating this area in the church visually communicates "You are welcome here. We want you and your children to worship with us. We absolutely expect that will come with the noise and movement children bring." The difference the children's area has made is extraordinary. From being a church with almost no children, I have received comments like "I had no idea you were so welcoming to families." "We love coming here, it's such a child friendly place."'

If you're thinking, 'That sounds like a great idea, but my congregation would never go for it', do carry on to the next few chapters for some ideas on managing change.

### Case study: The Benefits to the Whole Congregation

'When I arrived, there was a "children's corner" at the very back, entirely hemmed in by 4-foot-high barriers. Obviously that needed to change!

'One of the things I did early on in the process was to invite the PCC to gather in that area, and get down to the height of a child. Then I asked, "How do you know you are in church?" It was a light-bulb moment as they literally saw things from the children's point of view, and realized that they could neither see nor hear worship, let alone participate in it.

'Then I invited them to do the same in the space I wanted to move the children into, and asked the same question. They could see the altar, the pulpit, seasonal banners ... and the rest of the congregation!

'That move was transformational (although not without its hiccups along the way!). The children were surrounded from the start by the liturgy and by the worshipping community – in short, they were physically included in the church. That generation of children naturally began to participate more and more in the liturgy as they grew up.

'It also changed the way the adults perceived the children. Because they were physically worshipping alongside them, they began to view them more as fellow worshippers, and because they could see them, they began to consider their needs more.'

*Children's Worker, Diocese of Oxford*

The goal is to create a space that has room for everyone, like Noah's boat. Not just a small boat, exclusively for those special enough to Noah, but rather, like April said, a boat big enough for all the animals. A boat that can keep us safe from the storms outside, and feel like home. A boat in which we are not just stuck in the hold getting seasick but are free to enjoy the beautiful boat itself – to gaze in awe and wonder at the ocean and the sky, and to join in with what's happening on deck. A boat in which, as we nervously come up the gangplank, we can be reassured that yes, we belong here, there is space for us, we are safe and welcome, and included.

## Discussion Questions

1 What are the biggest physical barriers, in your church building, to being welcoming towards children and families?

2 What changes can be made? Which are most important? Which can be done relatively quickly and cheaply?

3 What are the needs, in terms of space, of families with babies? Toddlers? Primary-school children? Teenagers?

4 If you have children and families already present in your church community, how will you include them in deciding what to do and what the needs are?

5 How can you send visual signals to families that they are welcome in your church building? If someone walked into your church when nobody else was there, how would they know this is a place where children are valued?

6  Where do children spend most of their time? What does that place feel like? Is it clean? Does it feel like sacred space?

7  When children are in church with everyone else, where do they sit? What do they see/hear/smell from there?

8  What can children make that can be used in displays or in worship?

# 4

# The Dreaded 'Shhhhhh' and Other Cultural Barriers to Welcome

The Orthodox Bishop Anthony Bloom was apparently once asked, 'What shall we do with children in church? They interfere with our prayers.'

He replied, 'When you begin to pray, they will stop bothering you.'

What's behind this pithy, Twitter-ready quote is the fact that the journey from seeing children as a distraction to seeing them as welcome is one of spiritual transformation. And it's not about changing the children – it's about changing ourselves, so that our churches are a place where children can encounter God. That means changing our buildings, our perspective and our institutional culture.

One of the uses of the word 'culture' is in describing the development of bacteria. And in a way, that's an apt image – bacteria are invisible, but they get everywhere. Some can be very helpful and even life-giving. Some are harmful. The same is true of our institutional cultures.

Every church has its own mini culture, and denominations have their own culture as well. What are some of the cultural issues that may be getting in the way of your church being able to welcome children and families? And what can you do about them?

First, I'll look at a few of the most common issues that I've found in churches, and some of the specific things that can be done about them. Second, I'll look at a more holistic approach of how, in general, a church can be brought along on a journey of cultural change to be more welcoming and open to children and their adults.

## 'We'll come back when he's ready'

I grew up in the Episcopal Church USA, and in my diocese baptisms outside the main Sunday service were unheard of. They were a historical relic. The massive Victorian church I attended had a separate chapel with a baptistry; I remember being told it was where 'private baptisms' used to happen and being boggled that such a thing could exist.

Then I moved to the UK and I noticed that baptisms were often being held outside the main Sunday service. And I admit, my first reaction was not my finest moment. 'Oh, I see', I thought. 'They just want to use our pretty church as the background to their nice middle-class naming ceremony. They're not inter-ested in us as a community, or serious about joining. They're just exploiting us and we'll never see them again.'

I was wrong. And I realized I was wrong when I actually started working as a children's and families worker, and talking to the parents about why they were choosing a private ceremony.

Over the years, I heard dozens of parents speak about their fear and anxiety over bringing their children to church. And this held doubly true for a baptism, when they were worried not just about *their* kids but about their friends' kids, many of whom would have never been to church at all.

'My child can't sit still for an hour.'
'My child isn't ready for church.'
'My child will just disrupt everyone.'
'We're planning to come back when he's about five.'
'We want the christening to be after the main service, so we don't disrupt the congregation.'

The last one, especially, is hugely revealing. Parents coming to us for baptisms saw themselves and their children as unwelcome intruders on the peace and quiet of the people the church is *really* for, so they self-isolated. They were uncertain. They were self-conscious.

Many parents see themselves and their children as disruptive to the 'real' worshippers. I'll talk more about what's behind this later, but the anxiety parents feel is real and is keeping many children away from church. They want to raise their children in the church, they have a christening, and then life and fear get in the way – their toddler can't sit still; they may have a toddler and a newborn, but they intend to come back later when the children are a little older. Then, by the time their children are four or five, they've not got the habit of coming to church, and it never happens.

And yet the Mapping Practising Christians study found that 40% of adult Christians say they came to faith before they were five years old. Another 24% say it was between the ages of five and eleven.[44] So the majority of adult Christians became Christians before finishing primary school, and almost half before the age at which modern parents are even thinking about *starting* to bring them back.

Many parents themselves, looking back at the statistics from Chapter 1, grew up on the fringes of church, or with very little contact. They're not sure about what the rules are, when to sit or stand or kneel, what the actions and words of the service mean and what's expected of them.

Lydia, a priest and mum of two, told me, 'I was already ordained when I had my kids, so it was largely my husband who ended up with the joyful experience of trying to bring two small children to church every week. I don't think it was fun for him. For years, he was having to struggle with the reality of bringing two small children to church. And he was having to do it, because he was the vicar's husband – it's really hard bringing small children to church. Really really hard. And churches don't really realize that. They don't realize what it's already cost a young family to get there at all, what they've already contributed, the extra miles that they've already walked.'

Some of the suggestions in the previous chapter, about making a visually welcoming space and having a place where toddlers can engage in spiritual play during the service, can go a long way. But there are a few other changes that can help address parents' anxieties about coming to church:

---

44  www.comresglobal.com/polls/church-of-england-mapping-survey/.

- Some churches have started doing a 'teaching Eucharist' a few times a year. During this service, the leaders pause and explain what they're doing and why. It's done in a way that preserves the atmosphere of the service and the reverence, but aims to open up a bit of the mystery. Why do we face the Gospel when it's read? Why do the service leaders dress this way? Why does the priest wash her or his hands before communion? Why do we sit, stand and kneel when we do?
- Many churches have now learned to livestream services. Continuing to do this can give parents in your community the chance to find out, anonymously and invisibly, what worship is like, and more confidence to come into the building and participate offline.
- Have a notice in your service sheet or on the slide that's up as people arrive, saying something like:

> *Welcome to our service. If you're here with small children, we're very glad to see you! God put the wriggle in your kids, and we don't want to take it out. Please sit where your child can see and hear what's happening. We have a Pray and Play corner in the side chapel, which you can use. If your child needs some time out, you can use our hall – but please come back when your child is ready! As Jesus said, 'Let the children come to me.' To our worshippers here without children: children are a sign that the Body of Christ is growing, and a reminder that God is always doing a new thing. Please greet parents, carers and children with a smile, and a helping hand if needed.*

Or even posters made by children, like this one, made by Charlotte, aged eight. (Used with her permission.)[45]

---

45 Some great ideas on pew cards can be found at https://buildfaith. org/pew-cards-4-approaches-to-communicating-children-welcome/.

- Similarly, having a 'New to church?' leaflet in a place where it's easy to grab can be helpful. I've made two for the standard Church of England communion service – one for young children and one for adults and older children. You can download them here: https://stalbanscme.com/2016/04/25/welcoming-the-stranger/.
- Use the opportunities where you already have contact with parents to build their confidence in worshipping. Include some ideas on worshipping with children in your baptism preparation, where you have a captive audience. If you have a parent and toddler group with worship, use some phrases and actions that are similar to what you do on a Sunday, so

parts of the service are familiar, and invite them repeatedly to join you on Sunday morning.

- Find a few people who are really good at hospitality and encourage them to be on the lookout for new families, to coo over the babies, talk to the toddlers and reassure the parents that, yes, we are very glad you're here. These people may very well be teenagers or people of grandparent age.

- Say, repeatedly, from the front that this is a place where children are allowed and encouraged to be children, and to worship God in their own way. Hearing this can be validating to a parent who's a bit nervous.

- Use it as a signal from God. 'We've heard of one church', Ivy Beckwith and Dave Csinos write, 'that has transformed its responses to the fussing and crying of young children during worship. The congregation uses this "as a signal to pray for those in our world who are in need or cannot care for themselves".'[46] The cry of a baby is a cry of dependence, of a need that cannot be met by the baby alone. The response of a loving parent or carer is one that reflects a responsibility to care, and that builds trust in the child that this need will be met. Taking a moment to pray together for all the relationships where this bond of love, responsibility and trust exists, and for that part of our relationship with God our Father, can be profound.

But all of these ideas can only happen once parents and small children actually show up. To even get to that point you need repeated and regular invitations. Conventional wisdom in marketing is that seven contacts lead to one action – and this is even more true with sleep-deprived parents with chaotic schedules. Repeated invitations reassure anxious parents that,

---

46 Beckwith, Ivy and Csinos, David M., *Children's Ministry in the Way of Jesus*, Downers Grove, IL: Intervarsity Press, 2013, p. 76.

yes, you and your children are welcome. Yes, we really do want you here. It's okay.

In my discussions with young people on what makes them feel welcome, Jess, who is 17, said, 'Invite people to things, even if they don't come. So let's say someone comes to church all the time, and is just perfect, of course they'll be invited [to a church event] – but someone who doesn't come to church often, inviting them, I think they appreciate that, and it makes you feel welcome, and it makes you want to do stuff more.'

But in order for parents to feel safe coming to church, an invitation means there has to be something to invite them *to*. Is there a space for them and their children in church? Or are you only inviting them to something where they'll feel left out and unwanted?

Lydia, previously mentioned, told me about the journey one of her churches took towards alleviating the fears of parents and making it easy for them to come to church. It started with the congregation themselves:

'We looked at the promises right at the start of the baptism service – one of them is the church's job to welcome and uphold [children in their life with Christ]. Another is that the parents have a responsibility to "help their children take their place within the life and worship of Christ's church". And it's for the church therefore to provide a place that can be their place. And if there is no place that can be their place, how are the parents supposed to help their children find it?

'So we took those promises as our starting point, and we noticed that the church's promise is the first one, without which it's impossible for the parents to fulfil theirs. So frankly, if we say "they're using us, they're not keeping their promises", it's probably because we haven't kept ours.

'So we took that as our starting point and we critiqued everything we did around children in the light of [what it meant to] welcome and uphold [them], and what it meant to be the people of God. And we tried to develop a whole range of practices, not just around baptism but about what sort of places we were providing and creating for children and young families.

'And that meant that we ended up doing Junior Church differently, we ended up starting a monthly toddlers' liturgical service ... so that there was a place, and if people wanted to invite people to something, at least there was a "something" that was good for them, that they could invite them to, which then had continuity with Junior Church, because Junior Church had become more liturgical, which then had continuity with the All-Age Eucharist, because there were distinct patterns that were similar between all of these. There was never a leap between children's stuff and church – there was a continuity between different levels of participation and different inroads into the heart of the church.

'It was really hard work. And it took a lot of effort, much of it mine. But there were also really key people – and it was actually grannies, largely, who dared to take the risk, and facilitated a lot of this. They volunteered to be spare grannies – we matched up baptism families with old ladies, and in some cases old men, to give them a contact person who would get to know them before the baptism service, sit with them at the baptism service if they wanted, keep in touch with them afterwards, bring them pies ... babysit, get to know their children, all of that stuff.

'It all came from the liturgy itself. The liturgy contained within it all the challenge we needed to get us to do things differently.

'It was a massive, demanding journey, but a very good one – and without it we probably couldn't have ended up doing the All-Age Eucharist. That gave us the place to which we could invite people, but we already had to have done the shift in perspective to enable that to be a dynamic that could happen.'

Similarly, the Revd Lucy Davis, in Bedfordshire, spoke to me about the journey her church took around their baptism ministry. She emphasizes how the whole church used this opportunity to alleviate parents' anxiety about church as part of a deliberate strategic decision:

'It used to be that parents would approach us, we would prepare them for their child's baptism, have a lovely service, wave goodbye at the door and then be disappointed when they didn't return. But why should they return? Do we make it easy for them to return? Do we even invite them to return? And what would they be returning to?

'We communicate our welcome more clearly now; all families are now quite deliberately invited to come and join us one Sunday morning before we take a christening booking. A simple invitation to come, very often taken up, which says at a deeper level "This is not our church, this is your church too. This is not our God, this is your God too. You belong here. Christening is not a one-off, but is surrounded by the prayer and people of this place."

'And then, after the big day, more communication. More invitation. Another turning. Instead of lamenting the fact that we don't see families again, we now see it as our job to keep in touch with them. Yes, cards on the anniversary of their christening. But also more frequently too, using Mailchimp emails to stay in touch, letting families know about special services, about our toddler group, about Messy Church, about social events and fetes and Christingles and Christmas carols. And here is the thing: the majority of those emails are opened and read. We are not met with a wall of indifference. Far from it.

'So what has changed, where has this turning taken us? Into a new relationship with our christening families. Instead of quite literally providing a service, we are making relationships.'

So to encourage parents to come with your little ones, first you reach out. You invite, repeatedly. You reassure. You acknowledge the hard work involved in bringing small children to church, and make it as easy as possible for parents to feel like they belong. You provide a way for children to move and wriggle and still be in worship. And then you focus on building relationships.

We'll look a little more at this later on in the chapter when we consider the process of change. In the meantime, let's address another common barrier to welcoming children.

## Bouncy Castles, Memory Verses and Swimming Pools: What is Children's Ministry For?

Another cultural issue that often gets in the way of welcoming children fully to church is the idea of what children's ministry fundamentally *is* and what it's for.

In many churches, children's ministry is seen as a combination of education and entertainment. Children are there to be taught facts about God or to be seduced by a three-ring circus with magic tricks and a juggling show, with maybe a memory verse or moral lesson slipped in almost so they don't notice. What if your church saw children as being there to worship?

At the Household of Faith conference in 2013, John Westerhoff spoke about Christian nurture not as a process of education but as one of *enculturation*. It is, he argued, an anthropological exercise as much as an educational one. We learn what it means to live out our baptismal vows by being part of a community modelling the living out of those vows. This follows from his 2012 revised edition of *Will Our Children Have Faith?* in which he writes, 'For faith, it is therefore especially important to acknowledge that the most significant and fundamental form of learning is experience.'[47]

And when we look at everything else we do with children, that's the model we automatically follow. We don't lecture our children on art history before we allow them a paintbrush and paper. Ben Mizen, former Children's and Youth Advisor for

---

47  Westerhoff III, John H., *Will Our Children Have Faith?*, 3rd edn, Harrisburg, PA: Morehouse Publishing, 2012.

Portsmouth Diocese, points out that we don't make children stand next to the pool and watch adults swim, and teach them the physics of buoyancy, before we let them jump in. But also, we don't just throw them in the deep end and hope for the best – we give them water wings, and we stand next to them and help them figure it out. Barbara Meardon, former Children's Advisor for Salisbury, writes, 'We are called to be alongside as well as to model, to share in the journey of spiritual development … not as leaders … but as fellow seekers.'[48]

And yet somehow, when it comes to church, instead of letting children experience worship, and being alongside them as they do, we often teach them *about* worship.

Instead of letting them encounter God through story, prayer and music, we distract them with games that have nothing to do with the gospel and then try to sneak in a God bit in a way they won't notice, like adding pureed veggies to a burger.

Or we *try* to educate and entertain them, but we're uncertain about our own biblical knowledge, unsure how to teach and insecure about our ability to entertain, so we cheerlead them through a rendition of an action song, read a story from a children's Bible we picked at random, and then give them a colouring sheet to do. And we stress about whether they've gone away having 'got the message' about the story.

'How do I know they've understood the message?' is one of the questions I hear most often, from nervous children's leaders. There is a passion behind this question, a desire to ensure that children are engaging with the stories we're passing along to

---

48  Meardon, Barbara, 'Hoodie', in Sally Nash, Carolyn Edwards and Sian Hancock (eds), *Re-thinking Children's Work in Churches: A Practical Guide*, London: Jessica Kingsley Publishers, 2019, p. 112.

them. But I think the question is misguided because it comes from the belief that we're there to *educate* children rather than enculturate them.

Do we ask adults, as they leave, to regurgitate the main moral lesson of that week's Gospel? Do we get them up in front of everyone at the end of the service to share what they learned this week in church? Of course not. Because we all understand that adults are there to *worship*. But with children, we take a different approach. Instead of presenting the gospel as a mystery for them to explore, struggle with, play with, engage with and make meaning out of, we present it as a series of facts to be learned.[49]

As for entertainment, many churches *have* tried it with adults, especially among the megachurch movement in the USA, and it's spectacularly backfiring. Rachel Held Evans wrote in the *Washington Post*, 'You can be dazzled by a light show at a concert on any given weekend, but church is the only place that fills a sanctuary with candlelight and hymns on Christmas Eve. You can snag all sorts of free swag for brand loyalty online, but church is the only place where you are named a beloved child of God with a cold plunge into the water.'[50] She quotes a now-deleted blog post by the writer Amy Peterson, who says, 'I can be entertained anywhere. At church, I do not want to be entertained. I do not want to be the target of anyone's

---

49 Some children love facts. There are children's Bibles that are full of facts galore about ancient material culture and geography. Have a few of these books on hand. But don't feel that the children need to be able to recite the plagues of Egypt, in chronological order, or the exodus story of liberation, redemption and the triumph of the underdog, to mean something to them.

50 Rachel Held Evans, 'Want Millennials back in the Pews? Stop Trying to make Church Cool', *Washington Post*, 30 April, 2015, www. washingtonpost.com/opinions/jesus-doesnt-tweet/2015/04/30/fb07ef1a-ed01-11e4-8666-a1d756d0218e_story.html?utm_term=.71686b5c7166.

marketing. I want to be asked to participate in the life of an ancient-future community.'[51]

Children can be entertained by CBeebies, a trip to a theme park or even, for a two-year-old, watching the diggers at a construction site. At church, they can be invited to worship, to encounter the risen and living Lord through word and sacrament, to ask the big questions of life and try different answers. They can sing and make things, and serve one another. They can hear stories that will change them. They can walk alongside their siblings in Christ as we all seek together to live out our baptismal vows. That is what it means to be enculturated into church.

Here are a few examples of enculturation from my own ministry:

- How, at the start of Lent, we decorate a banner with the word ALLELUIA on it, which we then hide, as a reminder that we don't say this word during Lent. Secretly, the children and I remove the banner during Lent, decorate it with pictures of flowers and butterflies and eggs and other symbols of new life, and hide it again. It emerges on Easter Sunday transformed and beautiful. The children took on board the idea that Lent is a solemn time and you don't say the word ALLELUIA – so much so, in fact, that it began to be impossible to practise the piece we were going to sing at communion on Easter Sunday, as it contained that word and they flatly refused to say it. They basically went on strike. Eventually we had to replace it with 'pomegranate' during practice.
- The six-year-old who writes his name on the Gift Aid envelope and puts it in the collection plate because that's what he sees the adults doing. (He's learning something basic about stewardship there.)

---

51 Ibid.

- The ten-year-old who goes into the Pray and Play area, gets the chalice and pretends to give communion to his younger siblings.
- The four-year-old dancing her heart out to 'Alleluia, Sing to Jesus' in the aisle.
- The older woman who, of her own volition, goes to the candle stand and helps small children light candles safely after communion.
- The adults who invite the Youth Group to go with them on the local sleep-out to raise money for the homeless – showing them how their social conscience is connected to their faith, and their faith can be expressed through action.

All of these examples assume that children are at church not to learn a series of facts or to be distracted by a juggling act or magic show while we sneak God in before they can notice. They assume, instead, that children are to be taken seriously as fellow disciples; that children are at church to worship, just like adults. This is why I deliberately use the phrase *Christian formation* instead of *Christian education* to describe what it is we do.

In order for this to happen, we need to examine what concepts our congregation's culture holds about what children are and how they learn.

For much of the eighteenth and nineteenth centuries, children were thought of as blank slates, or empty glasses, who needed to be filled up with the knowledge and wisdom the adults held. These children were required to be seen and not heard; they were there to soak up what the adults gave them, and learn. Also, children were often seen as innately depraved by original sin – they needed to be corrected and brought to righteousness by being taught the message of the gospel. The primary need of children, in this model, was instruction.

Of course, we are not born knowing everything. And any honest reckoning of human nature must include the fact that we are also born with innate selfishness and other tendencies that we need to try and overcome throughout our lives. But this approach prioritizes obedience over authenticity, and assumes the child has no innate knowledge of, or relationship with, God. There is little trust in this model that God is already at work in the lives and hearts of children, or that children understand right and wrong.

So the image that replaced this was that of a seedling. In this model, the child contains everything needed for growth and development, but needs a nurturing environment and loving care, from the adults. Much of twentieth-century developmental psychology contributed to this understanding of childhood.

Starting in the late twentieth century, researchers began looking into children's spirituality – if development is predictable, the thinking went, and if spirituality is an innate part of who we are, then perhaps spirituality develops in predictable ways too. John Westerhoff and James Fowler developed theories of spiritual development, showing how children, or those newly converted to a religion, move through predictable stages. This also reflects the idea of the child as a seedling – we cannot expect a new seedling to look like a mature plant. The seed follows a predictable pattern from seed to plant, and you cannot rush the process or skip a stage. You have to accept the seedling as a seedling.

This model still encourages us to think of adults as those who *do for* children, however. We are still feeding and nurturing the seedling. Since the late twentieth century, some thinkers have begun to adapt the seedling model and think of ways it can be improved or changed. One of the images used in this thinking is of ourselves as fellow pilgrims, accompanying children on their journeys of faith.[52]

How we perceive children – as blank slates, seedlings, pilgrims – affects how we react to them.

If your congregation thinks children are blank slates, who need to be filled up with the wisdom we hold, they are more likely to view the sound made by children as a disruption, more likely to build children's programmes around teaching and learn-ing instead of worship and liturgy, and more likely to value, for example, memory verses, factual recall as signs of spiritual growth.

If your congregation views children as seedlings or pilgrims, they are more likely to view children as active participants in their own spiritual development, and see the adults' role as one of nurturing or accompanying. There is more power-sharing in the pilgrim model than in the seedling one, however.

But if your congregation holds a biblical view of children, they will see children differently. Because in the Bible, of course, children are more than any one of these models, or all of them.

- They are prophets (Jeremiah, Samuel).
- They are the first to glimpse the new life God offers, by being resurrected (Jairus' daughter, the widow's son – and the two children raised by Elijah and Elisha).
- They are signs to the community of God's promise of renewal and new life (Isaac, Obed, Jesus himself).

---

52 Much of the blank slate/seedling/pilgrim discussion is based loosely on material found in *Core Skills For Children's Work: Developing and Extending Key Skills for Children's Ministry*, Abingdon: Bible Reading Fellowship, 2006.

- They are crucial to Jesus' ministry (the child who offered their lunch at the feeding of the 5,000).
- They are examples of how we should be (the child in the midst).
- They are leaders (David, Jesus in the Temple).

Looking back at Lydia's example of helping her church figure out how to 'make a place' for children, you may want to begin by taking your existing congregation on a journey of examining the biblical view of children. This can be a sermon series, a Lent or Advent course (especially appropriate in Advent), a retreat day or any number of things.

You may find it helpful to ask your congregation to reflect back on their own childhood experiences of awe and wonder, and what those experiences mean to them and their faith now. (Be aware: you will need to have your pastoral hat on for this – not everyone's childhood is a happy place to return to.) By recalling that their own childhood spirituality was real, and not something foisted on them by adults, they can then be encouraged to remember that the same is true for children today. They are spiritual beings, on a journey, as we all are.

If you are reading this as a children's ministry volunteer, without the power to make something like this happen, and with a leadership hostile to it, you have a harder path. However, you can gather the volunteers, and whatever parents you have, and reflect on these issues and discuss how best to then trickle those ideas into the congregation at large. Are there parents represented on the PCC, for example? Would one be willing to stand?

Very often, the focus on education or entertainment comes from a place of anxiety – we have to cram all the knowledge in or they won't become Christians! Church has to be fun or they won't become Christians! But God is at work in children's lives, and our job is to nurture and accompany them, and give them stories and worship that will help them express and understand what's already happening.[53]

This same anxiety – concern for the viability of our faith tradition – can cause us to see children as an insurance policy for the future. Many well-meaning people have told me over the years that it's very important to welcome children to church because 'children are the future of the Church'. These people are often genuinely welcoming and open to children, keen to make relationships with them and committed to passing on the faith. But sometimes, in our concern to ensure our faith has a future, we forget that children are also the *present* of the Church. They are disciples of Jesus, right here, right now. They're just disciples who are a bit shorter than most of us, and think a bit differently.

Focusing on children as the future of the Church hides the often unrealized assumption that faith is something they will truly come to only when they're adults, rather than something that they have now. It assumes we're preparing them to encounter God as an adult, rather than accompanying them as they encounter God right now. It assumes we're more focused on who they will become rather than on who they are. And it can cause us to fret about whether they'll stick around as adults, rather than focus simply on being in the present moment with them.

It can be scary to make this leap. If we're used to keeping things light, or focusing on factual recall, or thinking about children

---

53 The seminal modern text on children's spirituality goes into the concept of this kind of trust, and its importance, in great detail – Nye, Rebecca, *Children's Spirituality: What it is and Why it Matters*, London: Church House Publishing, 2009.

in terms of the adults they're going to be, making the switch to 'We're going to maybe get into some serious stuff with kids, who are disciples worshipping right now, and there may be no right or wrong answers' is a big shift.

I spent one Sunday morning in late 2019 on the floor with a three-year-old and a five-year-old, as they repeatedly flipped the children's Bible page back to the picture of the crucifixion and asked questions about dying. It's scary. But it's incredibly worthwhile. It's a sacred place to be. And it's something you don't often get the chance to do at school, or in a place of entertainment.

And the thing is, if that's what our churches can be for children – not a place just to be educated or entertained but a place to be enculturated into a life as a follower of Jesus – then they'll know we take them seriously. They'll know we're a place where they can bring their anger, their sadness, their brokenness, their questions, their doubts. They'll know we're not just there to assess whether they know their memory verse or to fob them off with a bouncy castle instead of worship. They'll know we're being real, and they can be too.[54]

We'll talk more about children's spirituality and the scary things like death and questions about dinosaurs in later chapters. But for now, think about how your congregation views children and what the purpose of children coming to church is. Do they see them as there to be instructed? There to be entertained? Or

---

54 I feel I'm giving bouncy castles a bad rap here. I love a good bouncy castle. And I love sacred silliness. But bouncy castles and sacred silliness are a *side benefit* of being real and journeying through life together. They're not the main event. By all means, have a bouncy castle in your churchyard on Easter Sunday or at your Spring Fair. But don't have it *instead* of actual worship.

there to journey with us and learn, by doing, what it means to be a Christian?

## The Dreaded 'Shhhhhh'

About a year after I started as a children's worker, a lovely, supportive, wonderful member of the congregation approached me after a service. She put her hand on my arm and smiled.

'I think you do such *wonderful* work with the children', she said. It's always nice to receive praise, and I thought – brilliant! She's noticed the displays of their thoughtful responses to Bible stories. Or their contributions to our All-Age Services. Then she said, 'They're *so* much quieter now.'

This is often the big one, in terms of welcome. Parents stay away from church because their children might not be quiet. Worshippers may be hostile to the presence of children in church because they might not be quiet. Children who spend an hour on Sunday being told off for not being quiet might not be keen to go back.

And, as always, with a question of culture, there's a *lot* going on here.

So let's go back to the example from the last chapter, of the new family with a toddler, and take a close look at what might be going on under the surface, in the culture of a fairly mainstream church, that leads to this situation.

Imagine you're a parent with a three-year-old. You grew up going to church on special occasions but not every week. You've been to church for your wedding and for a few weeks around when your child was christened, but you felt self-conscious and worried about disturbing the *real* church members, so you stopped going.

Now your child is three and has heard some Bible stories at toddler group and nursery, and is asking questions about Jesus. You decide to go to church.

You are the only one of your friend group to do this, and you feel a bit weird about it. You and your partner have met the vicar of this church before, but know nobody else.

Despite being tired and overscheduled, you've got up on a weekend morning, dressed and fed yourself and your child, bundled them into the pushchair or car, gone to church and figured out where to put the buggy and where to sit.

The sign outside said 'ALL ARE WELCOME', but does that really mean you? It's so peaceful and contemplative here. Everyone seems to know all the rules. And here you are, in the back pew, unable to see or hear much of what's going on, trying to get your kid to sit still and be quiet. The backup toys and books and snacks you have in the nappy bag feel meagre and inadequate. The service will last about an hour.

Partway through, in one of the quiet bits, your child stands on the pew (is that allowed??) so they can see, looks at the stained glass windows, turns to you and says, 'Daddy, look, I see a sheep!'

In front of you, heads turn. Three or four people are staring at you. One of them says 'Shhhhhh'. A few others tut and not-so-subtly roll their eyes.

How do you feel?

Will you come back?

What message have you and your child just received about your place in God's house?

Let's unpack a bit about what's going on in this situation.

First of all, I'm immensely grateful to Carolynn Pritchard from the Spiritual Child Network for pointing out that there is a difference between *sound* and *noise*.

We all make *sounds* when we worship. There might be a 35-year-old who forgot to turn the sound off on their phone, and notifications ping up during the confession.

There might be the 84-year-old gentleman who is in denial about needing a hearing aid and is consequentially two beats behind everyone else when he sings.

There might be the 5-year-old who whispers observations to their friends about what's happening during the service.

There might be the teenager who turns to their grandparent during the sermon and asks a quiet question about what the preacher just said.

All of this is different from *noise*. Noise is genuinely disruptive.

Noise would be if your phone rang and you took the call instead of putting your phone on silent or going outside.

Noise would be a couple having an argument in the pew about whose family they're going to for Christmas dinner in a few weeks.

A child who is having a screaming tantrum falls under the category of noise, not sound.

And there needs, if possible, to be a safe warm place within the church building for parents to take children who need some time out. (They also need to be clearly told that we would prefer for them to *come back* when their child is ready!)

So yes, disruptive noise needs to be kept to a minimum in church. And yet, often, people react to any *sound* made by children – shouting 'AMEN!' at the end of prayers, calling their carers' attention to something in the building they've noticed, playing with a Bible-related toy like a Noah's Ark or a Nativity set – as though it were *noise*.

This is especially true in the case of children with additional needs, where regulating the sounds they make, the level of wriggling they need to do or the volume of their voice might be difficult.

James is the seven-year-old son of a friend of mine, and he has autism. I asked his mum if he would write me a letter about his experiences with church. Here's part of what he said:

'Mum and dad took me to church when I was a baby, but I stopped going for a while when I was about three or four. I didn't really know about how to be quiet then and I used to be really loud and jumpy when I was excited. I wasn't trying to be naughty, I just didn't know how to put my happiness into words. One day, a lady got cross with me for being loud and she yelled at mummy and mummy cried. That was really scary, so I stopped going to church.'

Compare this to the way a different congregation reacted. A clergy mum wrote to me: 'My son, who is on the autism spectrum, used to shout "boobies" over and over (we didn't know he had ASD at the time). I used to be in tears but somebody said to me that I must have the patience of a saint and encouraged me to keep coming.'

Both sets of parents were probably embarrassed and frustrated. The way the community responded is what made the difference.

In the second scenario, the embarrassment and frustration weren't ignored or punished – they were acknowledged. 'Yes, it's difficult', was the message. 'You're worshipping with a child who is doing something challenging. But we're glad you're here. You have patience. Keep coming back.'

It's difficult for parents to communicate that their child has additional needs when they're new to a church community. If a child is well known to a congregation, it's easier to understand what their needs are – but if we give parents coming to our church for the first time the benefit of the doubt, if we give them a smile and a helping hand or a word of encouragement, rather than immediately frowning because their child is making noise, we can make the difference to that family.

And flexibility is key. In James's new church, he says, 'Reverend Sue lets me take part when I can but also just do things in my own way with Mummy if I needed to. One day I had a melt-down, which I hate. It makes me feel like my brain is short circuiting. But no one told me off or anything and when I felt better they helped me join in. On the day I was meant to be reading but I felt too anxious so I did it with Mummy.'

But even apart from the particular needs of children with autism or ADHD or other additional needs, many churches treat the ordinary quiet sounds of children exploring church like *noise* rather than *sound*. Even if it's just a quiet whisper of 'That candle is really pretty, Mummy!' or a repeated 'AMEN!' into silence. Or the sound of a toddler's feet as they dance to a hymn or go to stand in the aisle so they can see the priest break the bread.

Why? Why do we shrug our shoulders at the elderly gentleman singing two beats behind, or the two mums having a whispered conversation on the way back from communion, while glaring daggers at children who are trying to worship and who are making no more noise than the adults are?

In my experience, I've found that this hostility towards children in church who are anything other than silent and invisible usually comes down to one of three reasons.

# 1 Pastoral reasons

For some people, the presence of children might be upsetting.

You might have just found out that your sixth round of IVF didn't work.

Your grown children might have told you that they don't plan to have children, and you're grieving the grandchildren you always thought you'd have.

You might be a parent whose child has died.

In this case, 'I've noticed you seem upset when children are around – are you okay?' can start a conversation about this behaviour. Often, when people feel able to express their emotions in a positive way, the passive-aggressive behaviour, and acting out, diminish.

The Revd Lucy Dallas suggests that even without a specific pastoral concern, adults may be hesitant to welcome children because of 'adult anxiety at children witnessing their emotions. Worship in church goes as deeply as people are willing to go – which is often much deeper than they might admit', she says. 'So this deep connection with emotional reality has to be contained within a "safe" context in order for adults to bear it, hence the uproar whenever any minister tries to change anything in worship. What children do is to burst in on adults' order, and just be children. It feels, I'd go so far as to say, like children running into the bathroom while adults are on the toilet. Adults are deeply ashamed of their emotional nakedness. So they keep the door locked.'

If this is what's happening in your church, then perhaps part of your journey needs to be towards becoming a place where everyone can allow themselves to open up more about their own emotions, even the complicated ones. How can this be done in pastorally safe ways? How can we reach out and trust each other, and become a community where it's okay to see each other cry or to express our deep emotions in healthy ways?

## 2 Fear and defensiveness

People may have an assumption about what a 'child-friendly church' looks like, and it's often some combination of a CBeebies show, a Viking raid and a children's birthday party, complete with clown and juggling act. (Again, this connects back to an assumption that church is there to educate or entertain children, not enculturate them.)

So when you say, 'We need to be more welcoming of young families', they hear, 'This church is going to turn into a three-ring circus of bright colours and loud noises and simplistic dumbed-down worship, and everything I love about my church, my spiritual home, will disappear. And what's more, I will be told off and called a crank for being upset about that.' No wonder they're defensive. I would be too, if that's what I thought was going to happen with more young families coming.

## 3 An unexamined, mistaken assumption about what church is

Gretchen Wolff Pritchard has pointed out that almost everyone, including parents and children themselves, comes into church with the unexamined assumption that children in church are 'guests at an adult event'.

This was driven home to me when I was at a rehearsal for my amateur dramatics group, which I automatically categorize as an adult event, and I got annoyed by the sounds made by an actor's three- and five-year-old grandchildren, who had come along. They were just playing quietly in the back, but I was trying to focus on the dress rehearsal, and I started rolling my eyes and internally tutting at their presence – which I would *never* do in church. Because in my mind, rehearsal is an adult event; that's for me. Church is a family event; that's for children too. But for many people, church is still in that first category – an adult event, for them, at which children are welcome if they can behave themselves and not disturb the people it's really intended for.

And this assumption is internalized by worshippers without children, parents and, often, by children themselves. So this is what happens:

> Worshippers without children think, 'Children are disrupting an event that's for me.' They may be more accepting at family events or other occasions where they understand it's for everyone.

> Parents think, 'My children are misbehaving and bothering the people who this is for. I'm embarrassed and I need to make them behave.' The emphasis then becomes not disturbing others, rather than engaging in the event.

> Children think, 'This is not for me. I have to sit down and shut up instead of being actively engaged, and wait until I'm set free at the end.'

The difference between children being *distracted so that they're quiet for others* and children being *actively helped to engage in worship* is crucial here. It's a large part of the thinking behind the shift from a Children's Corner to a Pray and Play area. And a huge part of it is reminding everyone – worshippers without children, parents and children themselves – that worship is a family event, not an adult event with children as guests.

These same parents, struggling to quiet their child at church ('An adult event; my child is a guest') probably behave differently at a children's puppet show ('This is for me and my kid together'). They engage their children, they make sure they can see, they whisper about what's happening, they make the experience sensory. Part of our role as church leaders is helping them realize that these same skills, which they probably already have, can be used at church. Sit where you can see. Whisper to your child about what's going on and what you think about it.

Carolyn Carter Brown's excellent Worshiping With Children blog has an article on 'Whispering in Church', which I started giving out to baptism families as part of the information pack during baptism prep. It includes such suggestions as:[55]

- Call attention to something that is coming; for example, 'This is the prayer where we all tell God what we're sorry about.'
- Suggestions about things to listen for, 'Jesus is going fishing in this story. What do you think he'll catch?' or 'There are a LOT of alleluias in this song!'
- Connect to something at home: 'My favourite blessing this week was our picnic yesterday. What was yours?'

I can almost hear the chorus of protest: 'I brought three young children to church every Sunday in the 1950s. Everyone did. It's just what we did. This generation is so precious and entitled. Kids need to learn to sit still and behave. Parents are too lax. If they bring their kid to church, that kid should behave. I grew up with the expectation that you learn to behave in church, and I'm fine.' So let's unpack this a bit.

There's a phenomenon called 'survivorship bias' that's partly at play here. One example is, 'Well, in the 1970s, we didn't have seatbelt laws or drink driving laws and we all lived to tell the tale. So clearly those things aren't necessary.' The problem is, people who *didn't* survive being driven around with no seatbelt by someone who'd just had ten pints aren't here to tell us about it.

---

55 https://worshipingwithchildren.blogspot.com/2012/10/whispering-in-church.html.

Similarly, in our churches, those for whom the focus on sitting still, listening to lots of words and behaving in the adult-orientated ways *didn't* connect them with God aren't in our churches to tell us about it.

When church was still a social expectation and obligation, those people may have dutifully still gone to church their whole lives, gritted their teeth and got through it. They may even have raised their kids in church, but there was probably a certain element of 'This is what we do on Sunday, it's our duty, so let's just do it and get it over with so we can have a nice roast dinner', rather than 'Let's go and encounter God and our fellow pilgrims through prayer, story, music and sensory experience.'

So as soon as it became socially acceptable *not* to stick around in church if it wasn't working for you, those people stopped coming. The only people left from those generations are the ones for whom that model of church worked. If it worked for more people who were raised that way, they'd still be here. But they aren't. So we need to do things differently.

That doesn't mean we need to throw out everything we love and value about our traditions. But we need to make sure there is enough flexibility in our churches for the following truths:

- Small children are wriggly and sensory. That's how God made them. That's how they discover the world, and that's how they discover God.
- There are a variety of different ways all of us, of any age, connect with God. Dave Csinos and colleagues interviewed children from a variety of churches and found that in general, they expressed their spirituality through one or two of four styles:

- Words (e.g. Bible study, discussion)
- Emotion (e.g. music, art, theatre)
- Symbol (e.g. imagery, mysticism)
- Action (e.g. activism, service).[56]

When I poll adults on which of these styles they most relate to, I get a variety of responses. Diversity in how we approach our diverse Trinitarian God is lifelong. Worship needs to make room for all these styles at various points. Not every part of every service will be for everyone, but as long as there's something there you can connect with, you can be included.

- People of all ages behave better when they are engaged and included. Anyone who's been to a children's recital will notice parents paying more attention when their child is performing, and possibly whispering to their spouse or playing on their phone when someone else's child is on stage. Why do we expect children who don't feel engaged to behave better than adults who don't feel engaged?

- With our children and teens knowing people of all faiths and none, questions and doubts are unlikely to be satisfied by 'This is what the Bible says; believe it and don't ask questions; trust the pastor because he knows better.' And there is less of a social penalty paid now for rejecting religion. Children who find their doubts and questions dismissed, and who are told to respect hierarchy and obedience instead, are unlikely to stick around.

---

56 Csinos, David M., *Children's Ministry That Fits: Beyond One-Size-Fits-All Approaches to Nurturing Children's Spirituality*, Eugene, OR: Wipf & Stock, 2011.

Unpacking the often hidden, invisible assumptions behind your church's culture can help clarify what's going on and provide insights on how to address it. Fear of change and a mistaken assumption about what church is, and what it means to be child-friendly, often lead to fear and defensiveness. When we drag these assumptions out into the open and challenge them, we provide the groundwork for moving forward and becoming more welcoming to children. Pastoral sensitivity will be needed for those whose unhelpful behaviour may be grounded in diffi-cult life experiences. Throughout, it is important to continually reflect on the role of children in Scripture, and the words of Jesus on children and childhood – this can help create a shared vision of how our churches can reflect God's abundant hospitality and love for children, and remind us all that whenever we welcome a child in Jesus' name, we welcome Jesus himself.

## Discussion Questions

1 Do any of these barriers to welcome sound familiar? Which ones?

2 How are children perceived in the culture of your church? As blank slates? Seedlings? Fellow pilgrims? Guests at an adult event? An insurance policy for the future? Some-thing else?

3 In the culture of your congregation, who is church con-sidered to be for?

# 5

# Boiling Frogs,[57] and Shock and Awe

I was recently working with a church who were considering various ways of changing their space and their worship schedule to be more welcoming to children and families.

There was a sense of frustration and defeatism.

'That won't work', was said over and over. I asked why. The response was always the same – because a certain group of people would throw a fit.

'It's just like with the kneelers', someone said. 'We spent a year, in PCC – a YEAR – fighting over what style of new kneelers to get.'

I said, 'That's because it's not about the kneelers. It's never about the kneelers. It's about *who gets to make the decision about the kneelers.*'

We like to think of ourselves as disciples of Christ, united in diversity, love and tolerance, but if you're reading this book

---

· 57 No actual frogs were injured in the writing of this book, and no frogs need be hurt in making changes to the culture of your church. All frogs referred to are strictly metaphorical. Please don't send me angry letters.

you're probably more familiar than you'd like to be with the power struggles among adults in church. And taking on any process of cultural change means confronting these power struggles at every turn.

Some clergy and children's workers have previous experience in the private sector, and many PCC members may be used to a corporate or hierarchical way of working. The boss is the boss. The boss and the governing body make decisions. A new boss comes in and may want to bring in their own people. They may find themselves frustrated when churches don't operate according to these rules, and try to force changes through.

Those who are trying deliberately to avoid this pitfall may end up going the opposite way and hesitate to make any changes unless *everyone* is on board. This can often lead to stagnation, frustration and the ability of one or two people to hijack the process for everyone.

Arlin Rothauge and Roy M. Oswald have done interesting work on how the size of the congregation affects the dynamic of a church and how it can change. Church growth tends to stall at certain predictable points, when breaking through a particular ceiling in terms of numbers means fundamentally altering the way that church operates. Churches with fewer than 50 active members are 'family' churches, 50–150 are 'pastoral', 150–350 are 'programme' and 350 and above are 'corporate'.

The role the clergy and leadership play are different in each – for example, once you hit a programme-sized church, it's difficult for one member of clergy to personally know every member. So you may find that you're visited in hospital by a lay pastoral care volunteer instead of the vicar.

Many of the power struggles over welcome towards children occur in family-sized or, to a lesser extent, pastoral churches – and these are the majority, at least, of Church of England churches.[58] This is partly because programme and corporate churches are more likely to already have significant numbers of children present – it's hard to reach 150 members just with adults. But it's also because the particular dynamics of the smaller church mean that power is often held by unofficial gatekeepers, whom Oswald refers to as the 'matriarchs and patriarchs'.

Rather dramatically, he sums up the dynamics of family-sized churches as follows: 'It is the patriarchs and matriarchs who control the church's leadership needs. What Family Churches want from clergy is pastoral care, period. For clergy to assume that they are also the chief executive officer and the resident religious authority is to make a serious blunder. The key role of the patriarch or matriarch is to see to it that clergy do not take the congregation off on a new direction of ministry. Clergy are to serve as the chaplain of this small family. When clergy don't understand this, they are likely to head into a direct confrontation with the parental figure. It is generally suicide for clergy to get caught in a showdown with the patriarchs and matriarchs within the first five years of their ministry in that place.'[59]

Because most Church of England churches fit this category, and most of the people I spoke with, and most of my own experi-

---

58 Source: Statistics for Mission, 2017, Median all-age weekly attendance: 35 people, www.churchofengland.org/sites/default/files/2018-11/2017StatisticsForMission_007_.pdf, p. 9.

59 Oswald, Roy M., 'How to Minister Effectively in Family, Pastoral, Program, and Corporate-Sized Churches'; https://static1.squarespace.com/static/54c7d7ede4b03a45e09cd270/t/5aa00b43652dea8c73c46299/1520438089615/HowToMinisterEffectivelyInFamilyPastoralProgramandCorporate-SizedChurches.pdf, p. 2.

ence in working with churches through the process of cultural change, are in this kind of church. For larger churches, there may be more moving parts to consider – for example, a school or nursery attached to the church may need to be brought on board, a larger team of volunteers may need to be consulted, a paid children's ministry team may be involved or decisions may need to be made about more formal existing programmes.

## Case Study

Trinity Church is in a wealthy home-counties town, with traditional worship. The town-centre church is about a mile away and has an excellent church school, so Trinity has always struggled to get traction with families. Ten years ago, they had an average Sunday attendance of about 60 to 80, with anywhere from 5 to 20 children, and the incumbent and PCC made the decision to hire a children's worker.

The main complaint from the worshipping community was that the children made too much noise and the parents didn't discipline them. Most baptisms were outside the main Sunday service and baptism families came to church occasionally afterwards or not at all.

In the first meeting after the children's worker was hired, the incumbent and children's worker thought together about what quick wins could be made. This resulted in a clear-out of the space one children's group shared with multiple adult groups, the purchase of new and better resources and a few small changes to the logistics of the Junior Church groups.

Over the first summer, the children's worker installed a Pray and Play area on a trial basis. The incumbent announced this was happening imminently, for several weeks before it went up. He explained to parents that it could be used to help their children stay in worship instead of having to be taken out, and that it would hopefully benefit the rest of the community by reducing the number of toddler meltdowns happening in church.

After the trial period, it was decided to keep the Pray and Play area, but move it to a different space within the church. It would need to not include permanent furniture, as the space it took up was sometimes used for seating during concerts, among other things.

A few parishioners complained that it ruined the beauty of the church, but most were relieved at the reduction in the frequency of toddlers screaming during worship. Parents expressed relief at having somewhere for their children to go that wasn't outside the worship space.

One parishioner repeatedly expressed dissatisfaction at the presence of children in worship and became passive-aggressive towards parents – especially new ones – and the children's worker. The incumbent spoke with this person and discovered difficult pastoral reasons behind their behaviour. The incumbent also worked to facilitate a positive relationship between this person and the children's worker.

The incumbent realized there were no parents represented on the PCC and spoke with several families – eventually, three parents joined the PCC. The children's worker was invited to attend four PCC meetings a year.

Junior Church was reworked to become more liturgical, so children would become familiar with the elements of the main Sunday service and the seasons of the church year. A space to display the artwork made by children in Junior Church was found in the area where the congregation shared coffee after the service, making them more visible. A fundraising campaign paid for accessible toilets, with space for a changing table and a nappy bin.

A few years later, a new incumbent arrived. This vicar was committed to All-Age Worship and doubled the number of All-Age Services happening throughout the year. The format of these services stayed close to the traditional style of worship the church was familiar with; however, services were a bit shorter, and often included more interactive prayer activities and preaching, different ways of presenting Bible stories (drama, video and so on), and leadership by people of different ages.

Children were trained as servers and greeters, read the lessons and often wrote the prayers. On one occasion, three members of the Youth Group gave the address. The director of music, and one member of the choir, started an ad hoc intergenerational orchestra, which often played at All-Age Services, with musicians ranging from age 8 to over 80. Changes were made to be in keeping with the church's liturgical tradition, but to push the boundaries bit by bit.

After a year or so of the new All-Age Worship schedule, the new incumbent and children's worker were surprised to find that adults were not only tolerating the All-Age Worship but speaking to the church leaders about what it had meant *to them*.

Elements of worship designed to be accessible to children, which took children's spirituality seriously, ended up being profoundly moving for adults as well.

Drama and prayers developed and written by children, expressing their own concerns and petitions, and their own ideas of how to present Bible stories, ended up being profoundly moving for adults to see and experience.

The adults had gone on a journey almost without realizing it – from considering children to be a distraction, and leaning on church leadership to keep them quiet, to realizing how the presence of children among the Body of Christ was enriching for all, and what it had to offer *them*.

No church is perfect. Trinity Church made mistakes – people left, volunteers got burned out, communication fell through the cracks, there were power struggles with the town-centre church and its school – but having watched part of their journey, and many similar ones over the years, I believe there are things they did right, which can be learned from. The journey they went on – from viewing children as a problem to be dealt with, to seeing them as a gift that enriches the church as a whole – is transformative. It's a culture change. We'll pick apart some of what they did in the remainder of the chapter, as it relates to the principles of change management

## What Not to Do

But first, let's start with a counter-example. How can you mess up the process of change? Many people reading this book will be all too familiar with the BBC Two sitcom *Rev*, which makes for sometimes uncomfortable viewing in its skewering of church culture.

In Series 1, episode 2, Adam – an Anglo-Catholic vicar who shepherds a small flock in East London – invites Evangelical pastor Darren to guest preach at his church one Sunday.

On Sunday morning, Adam walks into the church and finds it full of beanbags and fairy lights. There are screens at the front of the church.[60]

Here's what happens:

| | |
|---|---|
| **Adam** | Darren! |
| **Darren** | Hey – Adam! *(Looks around, shakes Adam's hand)* Pretty awesome, huh? |
| **Adam** | I didn't know you were going to do all this. |
| **Darren** | It's great, isn't it? I always like to joke that the more God loves you, the better your PA system. *(Uncomfortable laughter from both)* |
| **Adam** | I … haven't got a faculty permission for any of this. |
| **Darren** | Don't panic. Keep your cassock on. We will have it put back to the cold barn it was before. *(Uncomfortable silence)* Jesus is awesome, isn't he? *(Adam's wife, Alex, enters)* |

60 You can view this scene at www.youtube.com/watch?v=H1llKc RDXCU.

| Alex | This all looks good, Adam! A bit friendlier. Was this your idea? |
|---|---|
| Adam | Um, no. Let me introduce you to Darren, our guest preacher. Darren, this is my wife, Alex. |
| Darren | Hiya. |
| | *(Darren and Alex shake hands)* |
| Alex | Hi. *(Pointing at the screens)* Are people allowed to watch telly during the service today, Darren? |
| Darren | Did you do the, uh, flowers? I'm so sorry we had to … move them all out. |
| Alex | No, because a) I never do the flowers, and b) I was at work. |
| Adam | Alex is a solicitor. She does a lot of Legal Aid work. |
| Darren | Wow! Good for you. Not just a vicar's wife! |
| | *(Uncomfortable silence)* |
| | *(Darren looks at his watch)* People are going to be arriving in about thirty mins. Let's go help set up that smoothie bar! *(Darren exits)* |
| Alex | What [an idiot]. |
| Adam | It's fine, it's just one Sunday. |
| Alex | Though he is very good-looking … |

I often show this clip in training and ask people to reflect on what both Darren and Adam did wrong in making changes at this church. Here are some of the responses:

**Darren**

- Didn't tell anyone what he was doing.
- Made decisions unilaterally.
- Dismissed the existing worship and ministries (moving the flowers out, calling the church a cold barn).

- Made changes out of keeping with the church he was coming to.
- Made dramatic change, quickly.
- Dropped in and left – 'it's just one Sunday'.

**Adam**

- Got defensive and passive-aggressive.
- Immediately looked for problems ('I haven't got a faculty') instead of considering the benefits of the changes (even his wife said it looked friendlier).

As we're focusing on being the ones to make change, we're going to look mostly at how to avoid Darren's mistakes. If we avoid becoming Darrens, there will be fewer opportunities for people to become Adams.

# Darren's first mistake: didn't tell anyone what he was doing

If you came home one day and found that your partner had completely redecorated your home while you were out, even if you liked the new design, you'd probably be a bit upset that nobody consulted you. The same goes for redoing our spiritual homes.

The first step – and this underpins every step beyond it – is prayer. Don't make big changes without prayer. Prayer is how we communicate with God, and it's also how we communicate with each other. It's how we remind each other what we value as a community, and remind ourselves, and each other, that God is at the heart of what we do.

Pray with everyone involved, for wisdom and guidance – and start praying with your congregation for children. Praying every Sunday for the children in your parish, and the children in your congregation's lives, reminds them that children exist and sends a message that as we come before God in prayer, they are in our hearts, as a matter of routine. Make praying for children a habit among your congregation.

Prayer is also a way of gathering the congregation together with a united purpose, so that you're not, as Darren did, trying to make big changes on your own. To bring a community through a process of cultural change, you need to bring as many people as possible along with you. Sadly, there may be some people who cannot, ultimately, get on board with what the community is doing, and this is deeply distressing for everyone involved, but the goal is to minimize the frequency with which this happens. Give everyone as much of a chance as possible to be an ally.

This means announcing ahead of time what's going to happen, so people have a chance to get used to it, to ask questions about it, to share their thoughts with each other and with the leadership, and to learn more. If your PCC has decided to switch Junior Church from every week to twice a month, your Junior Church leaders should not hear about this at the same time as everyone else. And, ideally, they should be involved in making that decision in the first place.

And you may need to spend a lot of time listening to fear, frustration and, yes, criticism of you and your plans. This can be hard. But if you are not open, and willing to communicate, you create an environment that is ripe for rumour-mongering, passive-aggressive lashing out and sabotage. This is even more unpleasant.

Also, it means providing opportunities throughout for people to learn more, and checking in with how the process is going. Providing training, regular open meetings and one-on-one time with anyone who's learning a new skill or approach ensures that you keep communication open throughout the process – you don't just announce what's going to happen and then close the door.[61]

Open communication is also how you inspire your congregation that welcoming children and families is something exciting, profound, life-giving and beneficial to the whole body of Christ.

While churches often have an aversion to anything that feels corporate or managerial, it's useful to look at models used in the business world for managing the process of change. One of these, called the 'ADKAR' model, put forward by Jeffrey Hiatt, emphasizes that for an organization to change, *people* have to change.[62]

Hiatt focuses on Awareness and Desire as the first crucial steps to change. First, you have to be aware that you need to change, but then second, there has to be the *desire* to change. Separating these two steps can be useful – often, we skip straight from 'There's a problem!' to 'What do we do about it?', and that means we can leave people behind who could be brought along with us, creating unnecessary conflict.

---

61 Some of these points are taken from Kurt Lewin's 'unfreeze, make changes, refreeze' theory of change management. You can find brief summaries of this, and a few of the other ones I refer to, as well as some I don't, at www.process.st/change-management-models/.

62 The five steps in the ADKAR process are Awareness, Desire, Knowledge, Ability and Reinforcement. Find out more at www.prosci.com/adkar.

Most of our churches have the *awareness* part down pat; we can see how few children we have but, apart from one or two people, the genuine desire to change can sometimes be slow to follow. We put off the problem to another day. We kind of like the peace and quiet of having an adults-only space. We're aware of the problem but we have no real motivation to change.

In this model, the desire for change has to bring both the emotional and logical sides of the person on board.[63] Many churches may have the logical side of the desire sorted – we know we need more children, we know it's a good thing, but the culture of our church may still look upon it rather like a child told to eat their vegetables. We know it's good for us but we don't like it; so we do it because the authority figure tells us to but our hearts aren't in it. Because, yes, our logical side knows that children are the future of the church and we need them for the good of the church, but the emotional side – the fact that children are good news, that they are the *present* of the church as well, that we are all richer when the whole Body of Christ, of all ages, is there – hasn't caught up.

How can you create that desire for change in your church? How can you begin to show what a gift the presence of children is and how much better the community will be when children and families are present?

---

63 Ibid.

## Darren's second mistake: made decisions unilaterally

Another theory of change management, devised by Professor John P. Kotter of the Harvard Business School, focuses on the importance of building a core group who can then form a strategic vision and get everyone on board.[64] (The first step, before that, is 'create a sense of urgency', which your national church leaders, Statistics for Mission in hand, are probably already doing for you. So you've got that covered.) Darren singularly failed to do this.

The obvious place to begin forming your core group is your PCC or church governing body. This is where the Revd Robb Sutherland, a vicar in the Diocese of West Yorkshire and the Dales, began. 'We sat down and talked about the place of children in worship', he says. The benefit of this was that 'having a large group of people in church who understand the aims of growing the Kingdom of God means that there is someone in each area of the church who can spread the good news of children across the whole congregation. If someone tuts and says 'Shhhhhh' it's much easier for one of their peers to just say "They're okay, they're just playing" than for me to say it.'

Robb also points out that there's an added bonus to having a group approach. 'I now have a large group of people on the look-out for faith-based toys wherever they travel. It means that I get handed lovely things like a wooden Nativity jigsaw for toddlers with "I saw this in [insert northern seaside town] and thought the children could play with it."'

---

64 Kotter, John P., *Leading Change*, 2nd edn, Boston, MA: Harvard Business Review Press, 2012.

Having a group like the PCC or a children's and families working group means you have a task force ready to take this on. It means you're not setting up 'the vicar/children's worker/ whoever versus the rest of us' or putting the entire burden of changing the culture on one person.

If you're forming a working group or putting your PCC in charge of this task, think carefully about who should be included. Are there nurseries or schools, uniformed organizations or other groups your parish has connections with, where children are present? How can they be included? Do you have any parents on your PCC? Can you include older children or teenagers in your working group, or have a 16- or 17-year-old on your PCC? Who is most opposed to the types of changes you'd like to make? Should they have a seat at the table?

Making sure your working group or PCC is as diverse as possible helps avoid the phenomenon of groupthink. Groupthink is a social psychological phenomenon in which conformity among a group reinforces irrational – or even harmful – decision-making. Groupthink tends to occur when the following are in place:

- High group cohesiveness: 'We are the enlightened in-group and have all the right ideas.'
- Structural faults: the group is insulated from alternative viewpoints, similar in background and ideology, and has a leader whose views and preferences are well known.
- High external stress: there is pressure to make decisions or show results, recent failures and a fear of being seen to make wrong decisions.

Groupthink has been shown to actively suppress dissenting viewpoints, underestimate risks and overestimate certainty of success. Group members report a tendency to self-censor when they fear their ideas don't meet the group's norms, and pressure to conform is often couched in terms of morality or disloyalty (e.g. 'I suppose you just don't care if the church dies, if you're not willing to get on board with having All-Age Worship every week').

Ensuring that you have a variety of viewpoints present in your group, providing space deliberately for people to critique ideas, breaking the group up into smaller groups for part of the discussions, and the leader absenting him or herself for some of the time can be helpful in breaking these often invisible barriers to good decision-making.[65]

John Kotter and Holger Rathgeber, in *That's Not How We Do It Here!* also point out the importance of a group taking time to 'collect some ideas … not comment on any yet. First, just collect them.'[66] Allow space for all ideas, no matter how weird or seemingly daft. This can help prevent self-censorship ('No, I won't speak up, that's stupid') and encourages creativity. And you never know – the completely daft idea may spark a different idea, which in turn sparks another, which gets you to where you need to be.

However, you may decide that forming a core group or beginning with the PCC wouldn't work for your church, and you want to start with a whole-church approach. Or you may want

---

65 I first learned about groupthink as a psychology undergraduate, from David Myers' textbook *Social Psychology* – the most recent edition is co-authored with Jean Twenge, and is the 13th edition, published in New York in 2018 by McGraw Hill Education.

66 Kotter, John and Rathgeber, Holger, *That's Not How We Do It Here! A Story About How Organizations Rise and Fall – and Can Rise Again*, London: Penguin Random House, 2016, p. 65.

to begin with the whole church and form a working group or core group later.

Starting with the whole church has the advantage of making your process and decision-making as open and transparent as possible – and if someone chooses not to engage, they can't say they were deliberately left out.

Having an open meeting, to which everyone is invited, can also be an opportunity to confront the often hidden, invisible rules in your church's culture. You can cooperatively put together a vision statement or a list of core values (start with the Beatitudes? Ten Commandments? baptismal vows?) and use that as a guide in your decision-making, priorities, and in discussions about the behaviour of groups and individuals ('Does the way we act at coffee time after church reflect the suggestion just made about making welcoming the stranger a core value?').

Having the whole church create this vision and take ownership of it means that responsibility for it lies with the whole congregation. And if the hidden, invisible parts of your culture end up clashing with it, you now have something to point to, to which everyone contributed, to challenge the hidden invisible culture.

And there is another benefit as well to starting with the whole church – as Robb Sutherland pointed out, people may listen to their peers more than to the leaders.

In my role as a diocesan advisor I was working with a church considering admitting children to communion before confirmation. The vicar and I facilitated an open PCC meeting, which was attended by many members of the congregation. One woman spoke passionately about her belief that opening communion to younger children cheapens the sacrament and makes it less important and special. (I don't share this opinion, but it's a legitimate one to hold.) The vicar was about to jump in and present an opposing argument, when another church member took the microphone instead. She spoke quietly and eloquently about her belief that opening communion to younger Christians connects them deeply to God in an important way.

Afterwards, the vicar told me, 'I don't think she would have heard that argument if it had been me who said it. She would have tuned me out, because I'm the vicar, I'm pushing this process, she knows my agenda, and I come with hierarchy and authority that she's pushing against. But because it was Debbie who said it, I think she was open to hearing it.' I don't know if she changed her mind. But it made for a better discussion than if it had been the vicar saying it.

Talking about what your church is going to do – a deliberate stocktaking, making change and reviewing in order to create a culture that is welcoming to children and families – gives your congregation time to prepare. It gives them a chance to catch the vision and to share with you any concerns and misgivings they may have. Keeping communication going throughout gives you the opportunity to repeatedly check in with them about what they need from you, how the changes are going and what training or support your staff and/or volunteers may need.

Even with decisions that are being made by the leadership, fairly unilaterally, you can bring people into the process. Ruth Harley, an ordinand and former children's worker, explained that when introducing changes to a congregation, she always says 'We're going to *try* ...' instead of 'We're going to *do* ...'

And it's as much for the benefit of the leaders proposing the change as it is for the congregation.

'People are often fearful or apprehensive about change', she says. 'But they may well be willing to give something a go, if they don't feel that they are committing to it permanently, or being forced into it. "We're just trying this today/this month/ during Lent" is a great way of lowering the stakes, both for those proposing change and those who might oppose it.

'If it doesn't work, that's fine – we tried. Nobody's staking their reputation on it. Similarly, by allowing the possibility of trying something new, people don't feel they are committing themselves to something unknown or abandoning something they have held dear.

'The other great advantage of "just trying it" is that it feels more collaborative. We are on a journey of experimentation and discovery together, rather than something being imposed by one person or a small group on others against their will. The humility of saying "I don't know if this will work, but let's give it a go together" opens the door for those who might otherwise have been our staunchest opponents to have the humility to say "Actually, that's not so bad" or even "Actually, I quite like that after all" without losing face.'

The magic of 'try' instead of 'do' defuses part of the power struggle. If you've spent huge amounts of social capital forcing a change through, because you think it will be good for children and families, and then it doesn't work, backtracking is embarrassing for you – and it can also hand a huge amount of power to the people who opposed the change. 'See, Father Bob, I told you it wouldn't work. I was right that we should stick to the way we've always done it.'

However, in order for 'try' instead of 'do' to work, you have to genuinely be open to receiving feedback from people who may disagree with the decision. Otherwise, the idea of a trial period is simply a sham, and people will realize it and become even more upset and oppositional.

Trinity Church's trial of a Pray and Play corner resulted in making the change permanent, but also in some adjustments to where it would work best and how flexible that space would be. This was in response to feedback – some of it from people who had been most sceptical of the idea. By saying 'Yes, you're right – the Pray and Play corner is *not* working in that space', trust was built between the church leaders and the sceptics, that the sceptics would be listened to and included.

The first incumbent at Trinity also did something very important – setting up initial quick wins that would help gain the trust of people sceptical of change. The first big, visible action of the children's worker was to make the area shared by children and adults a much nicer, cleaner space. This worked for everyone – the children had better resources and the adults had a less cluttered and overwhelming space. By showing the sceptics among the adults, 'This can be good for *you* too', the incumbent helped get them on the side of the changes he wanted to make, and set his new employee on a positive foundation with the congregation.

But no matter what you try, you may receive criticism. In receiving criticism, and making decisions following a trial period of a change, these are some things to keep in mind:

- What emotion is underneath this criticism? What is this person *really* saying – fear, anger, defensiveness, marking territory?

- If they're stating their criticism in an unhelpful way, how can we, as leaders, separate our emotional response to this from any legitimate point(s) they may be raising?
- Is now the best time to have this conversation? Should we make an appointment to meet and discuss it at a better time?
- Am I the best person to discuss this with them, or is there someone who has a better relationship who should be brought in?
- Is there a win-win solution anywhere? Can we avoid 'It's your needs vs the children's needs' and find something that works for everyone?
- Is this really about the kneelers or about who gets to make a decision about the kneelers? Don't waste time rebutting argument after argument when the arguments are simply a mask for a power struggle. (See also the first point: if it's about fear of change, don't get dragged into a two-hour conversation about kneeler colours. Reassure and address the fear instead.)

## Darren's third mistake: dismissed the existing worship and ministries

Another mistake Darren made was showing that the existing ministry of the church and its traditions didn't matter to him, by referring to the building as a 'cold barn' and moving the flowers (which were someone's offering of time and talent) out of the sanctuary. When managing change, it's important to acknowledge and celebrate what has gone before in the community, and the people who hold the community's history.

When change happens, the message the old guard often receive is, 'You're not valued any more. Your time has passed. You're holding us back. Get out of the way and let us do it our way now.' Hearing that doesn't feel good. And, crucially, even if you haven't said it or implied it in any way, when people hear the word 'change', they may *expect you to say it, and react as though you already have.* Extra care and sensitivity needs to go into reassuring people who may feel they have something to lose from changing the culture of your church.[67]

Another model of change management, put forward by William Bridges, focuses on the emotional and psychological response to culture change, and how to manage that. This model begins with a process of 'ending, losing and letting go'.

Any change involves loss, and this brings out strong emotions – especially when change is happening in a place as full of emotions as one's spiritual home. The William Bridges Association's website describes this phase as one in which 'people identify what they are losing and learn how to manage these losses. They determine what is over and being left behind, and what they will keep. These may include relationships, processes, team members or locations.' If you have communicated clearly, made yourself available and created a strong positive vision of why the change is necessary and how your church will benefit, you will be well placed to guide your church through this stage.[68]

---

67 I could go on for pages about when this caution needs to be ignored because what you have to do is too important to wait to bring people along, or when the old ways of doing things are causing or enabling ongoing damage. Safeguarding is one example. For example, if a person, or a system designed to protect people, is actively and urgently in danger of harm, and the old guard is enabling a dysfunctional pattern of harm, then go ahead and shove them out of the way.

68 A brief summary of the three stages of Bridges' model and how to guide people through them can be found at www.mindtools.com/pages/article/bridges-transition-model.htm.

Sensitivity and reassurance are especially important if you are asking people to change the roles they're playing in church – reducing Junior Church from every Sunday to once a month, for example, or asking someone to step aside and make room for new blood, or to change their approach to leading sessions or worship. Bear in mind you are asking a lot of them. This is probably something important to them, which they have put thought, imagination, creativity, time and passion into over the years. Unless their behaviour is actively dysfunctional and toxic, they should be included in any decisions about how to change things, and have opportunities to continue offering their gifts in a way that works for everyone. Work with your existing leaders to address such questions as:

- What new skills are needed among children's ministry staff and volunteers?
- What new skills are needed among other areas of ministry? For example, do the greeters or clergy need to learn new things?
- What skills aren't being used effectively? (This can include the skills that children and young people themselves have to offer.)
- How do the systems and structures of the church need to change?[69]

One way of facilitating this is to go as a team to training on new techniques and approaches to children's ministry, and use the car or train journey home to share your thoughts and find as much consensus as possible. This puts you on an equal footing as learners, rather than in a hierarchy. It can also show that

69 These questions are adapted from the McKinsey 7-S theory of change management, first formulated in Peters, Thomas J. and Waterman, Robert H., *In Search of Excellence: Lessons from America's Best-run Companies*, New York: Harper & Row, 1982.

you're willing to try things that are new to you as well, and build trust.

If there is someone whose behaviour is genuinely toxic and is causing active harm to the agreed goals, ensure they know that they need to change or they will be asked to step aside, *before* you tell them they need to step aside. Offer training or mediation. Bring in the archdeacon or your denomination's outside authorities if needed. Give them every chance to change before it comes to confrontation.[70]

And if someone does ultimately decide, of their own accord, to step aside from a role, make sure you find a way to honour what they've done over the years. Share the stories of how their ministry has made a difference, give them a gift from the congregation and ensure, as far as possible, that their service is acknowledged and appreciated.

# Darren's fourth mistake: made changes out of keeping with the church he was coming to

Adam, in *Rev*, wears a cassock while walking around his parish. His congregation are used to quiet and contemplation, incense and traditional music. Darren appears in jeans and a waistcoat, and fills the sanctuary immediately with fairy lights, beanbags, screens and a smoothie bar.

No wonder they're a bit taken aback. It's called 'culture shock' for a reason.

---

70 Again, this does not apply if they are actively harming people or creating an unsafe environment.

You may have any number of magnificent ideas for changing your space, your music, your prayers, your Bible study programme, the format of your fellowship time and everything else (especially if you're a new children's worker or incumbent). But just because you love liturgical dance accompanied by 80s synth-pop and flashing coloured lights doesn't mean your congregation in a small village in the home counties, with an average age of 84, will feel the same. Similarly, if you're coming to a large Evangelical church with a worship band and 45-minute sermons, don't expect them to love it when you introduce weekly Benediction and carry a statue of Our Lady up the aisle, wearing a biretta (you, not the statue).

This truth applies just as much to changes you make to be more child-friendly. 'Child-friendly' or 'family-friendly' is *not a style of worship*. There can be Anglo-Catholic child-friendly worship, Alt-Worship child-friendly worship, Charismatic Evangelical child-friendly worship, child-friendly Forest Church or Café Church, child-friendly meditation, child-friendly Taizé and everything in between.

Remember that many of your congregation are probably operating under a number of the assumptions discussed in the previous chapter. They may, consciously or unconsciously, be assuming that being more child-friendly means dumbing down worship, filling it with nothing but action songs and magic tricks. They may believe, without even being aware of believing it, that children are here to learn or be entertained rather than to worship, and they may be afraid that if the old guard dislike any changes being made, they'll just be told to stop being cranks and get out of the way.

Hopefully you're doing some things to unearth and address these assumptions and challenge them, but alongside that, making changes to worship that are, at least *somewhat*, in keeping with the existing tradition of your church can be very reassuring.

Imagine it like sibling rivalry – these new, younger people are coming in and taking up Father and Mother's attention, and there's a fear you're going to be pushed aside and replaced. Just like new older siblings when a baby is born, existing congregation members may need to be reassured, through action, that the important things will still be there. They will still be welcome. They will still be loved. The family is still the family. It's just that we're making room now for some new members. Of course the new members will change us, by being who they are, but we're still the same family.

There are very many books on All-Age Worship out there, and many resources online as well. I've included a Resource List at the end of this book, where you can start looking for ideas. Ideally, you will find inspiration and ideas for making worship more accessible to children without dumbing it down, which push the boundaries of what your congregation is used to but are not unrecognizable to them.

For example, the director of music at Trinity Church, when she started the ad hoc intergenerational orchestra, stuck mostly to classical and folk music. Children were taking on a leadership role in worship – which was new – but in a way that was still recognizably that church's worship style.[71]

What you're aiming for, at this point, when you've got enough of the community tentatively on board with making changes and have started to make a few, is for them to leave your

---

71  We'll talk further about giving young people more power later on.

services going, 'Oh, *that's* what you mean! Oh. That wasn't too bad, actually.'

If you're making a more dramatic change, this school of thought suggests you scrupulously keep everything else the same. By all means go ahead and use a video in a church that's never used a screen before, but don't also use that same service to try interactive prayers, liturgical dance, lots of new music, mood lighting, a smoke machine, live animals and Stormzy's 'Blinded By Your Grace' played over a PA system during communion.[72]

You will still receive strongly worded emails, no matter what you do, often about the most surprising things. This is where all the previous 'We're going to *try* ...' stuff, and a sense of perspective, come in handy. You also need to decide which hills you're willing to die on, and pick your battles accordingly.

And again, remember to use groups. Where possible, changes to worship, and reviews of what worked and what didn't, should be done with at least a few minds working together. You get a more honest perspective on what works and on what's worth fighting over or can be let go. It's easier to deal with mistakes and criticism when you're taking it on as a group instead of focusing it all on one person. (Again, if possible, some of the people you consult should be parents, children and young people themselves, even if you can only make it happen occasionally.)

You can also make changes not to the service itself but to what you provide for young children and newcomers to help understand what's going on. I've mentioned a few of these before – the

---

72 To be fair, except for some types of live animals, most of these are brilliant ideas. But it might be a bit of a shock to get them all at once if you're not used to them.

'What Happens At Church' leaflets,[73] a 'Worship Clock' with pictures of what happens and a dial children can turn, teaching Eucharists (see previous chapter),[74] notes in your service sheet or any number of ways to make the strange things we do together on Sundays a little less abtruse. I think of it as a bridge – you're trying to bring the service a bit closer to where people are, and to bring people a bit closer to where the service is.

## Darren's fourth mistake(?): made dramatic change, quickly

I've put a question mark in this one because I'm now going to confuse you all by simultaneously arguing both sides of a point – is dramatic, quick change a mistake?

There's an old urban legend used to illustrate the process of change, which is where this chapter gets its title. If you drop a frog directly into boiling water, the story goes, it will immediately jump out. It's not stupid. It realizes it's being boiled alive.

But if you put a frog into cold water, and you gradually turn it up one degree at a time, the frog will get confused. It won't know when to jump out, because there's no single clear point when it goes from being safe to being boiled.

So with patience, eventually, you can have yourself fresh boiled frog's legs.

---

73 Leaflets at https://stalbanscme.com/2016/04/25/welcoming-the-stranger/.

74 The 'How2Charist' resource is an online taught Eucharist – you can use it in Youth Groups, in worship itself and so on. Find it at https://how2charist.com/.

I'm sure frogs don't actually behave like this, and I have no idea where the story originated, but the metaphor has some truth to it.

You try one small change. The congregation goes, 'Okay, this isn't so bad ...'

You give them some time to get used to it.

You try another small change. The congregation goes, 'Okay, this isn't so bad ...'

You give them some time to get used to it.

You try another small change. It doesn't work. You undo it, but because you did it separately from the first two, you don't have to tear the whole thing down and start again.

You try a fourth small change. The congregation goes, 'Okay, this isn't so bad ...'

Repeat as needed. Boiled frogs.

This is how I ended up, after seven years, with a very traditional, largely elderly Church of England parish at an All-Age Service, praying together using Lego. Yes, all of us. Seven years earlier it would have been unthinkable.[75] Six months later, our Reader preached at an All-Age Service and had them ... *talking to each other during the sermon*. To quote the sitcom *Home*, 'What you want is softly softly catchy monkey. Not *Planet of the Apes*.'

---

75 This is what we did, at http://flamecreativekids.blogspot.com/2015/03/lego-or-duplo-prayers.html.

In psychology, this is referred to as the 'foot in the door' technique, and it's a strategy used in sales as well as in many other scenarios – some good, some bad. It can be used to help someone build positive behaviours, but it can also be used to help people get used to committing atrocities. Psychological truths are neutral – it's how we use them that counts. If someone agrees to go shopping for ingredients with you, it's easier to get them to agree to cook the meal for you than if you'd started with the big ask.

A vicar in the Midlands told me about her church, which had resisted, for years, admitting children to communion before confirmation. She worked on including children in other ways – meanwhile, eventually, the PCC went through the process of admission and received the Bishop's licence. So finally, they had a cohort of seven-year-olds beginning to receive communion.

But by that time, 'Children were already taking a full part in ministry. They were reading, they were leading worship in various other ways, writing prayers.' So people almost didn't notice they were now also taking communion. By slowly asking for one small thing, then another, you reduce resistance to the big thing.

However, the Revd Edward Green, a vicar and one of the founders of the creative worship collective Sanctum, disagrees. 'Shock and awe is the best change management strategy', he says, half-jokingly. His argument is that sometimes big changes are needed to help change people's minds. 'Fast and large change enables people to see the immediate benefits. It brings a wow factor', he says.

And there's something to this – when Alex walks in to the church in the scene from *Rev*, she's wowed by the changes to the space. The church looks friendlier! Much better! She can immediately see the benefits of making change, which might not have happened if someone other than Darren had gone slowly and carefully. 'The church may be used to A', Green says. 'But you may well know that A will not do the job and C would be the better option. Rather than sell them B, which is a compromise, you wait until it is completely obvious that A will not work. Then C becomes the only option.'

Shock and awe can also be useful as a way of getting people to agree to something they would previously never have considered. The corollary to the 'foot in the door' technique is what's called the 'door in the face'. This is when you ask for something huge, knowing it will be refused, and then ask for something smaller. An example might be:

The person might have said no if you'd started with the second ask, but now, in comparison with the first, it feels minimal.[76]

---

76 Again, I first read both of these compliance techniques in psychology textbooks almost 20 years ago, but you can find a brief summary at www. simplypsychology.org/compliance.html.

So if you think shock and awe might be the way of breaking an impasse, you may as well go all out. Bring in the smoke machines, live animals, strobe lights and more. And then when your congregation – who would never have agreed to the smoke machine if you'd started there – says 'The smoke machine was brilliant, but can we not have the chickens everywhere?' you can happily agree.[77]

Perhaps your church may need a bit of both – in some areas you may want to boil frogs, working with the 'foot in the door' technique, and in others you may want to go for shock and awe, with the 'door in the face' technique. Each context, and each community, will differ.

Kotter and Rathgeber discuss a similar approach that's a bit of both in *That's Not How We Do It Here!* Organizations that are too rigid, structured and bureaucratic cannot respond quickly to change. Organizations that are quick and agile and non-hierarchical can become chaotic once they grow large enough.

They suggest a process of change that allows for both leadership (inspirational, creative, motivational people) and management (planning, budgeting, organizing and overseeing people). This distinction can be very helpful – often, organizations blend the two roles into one, without seeing that they require different skills. Who in your church are the leaders? Who are the managers? Is there a culture of expecting the vicar or children's

---

77  In response to a flippant Twitter comment about this, I have heard from multiple churches who have actually successfully used live chickens as part of worship, as well as one where the vicarage hens are free-range and keep wandering in randomly during worship. There is also the @mystic_chickens Twitter account, which pairs photographs of chickens with quotes from Christian mystic writings. Clearly there is an amazing untapped potential for chicken-inclusive worship.

worker to be both? What needs to change in how those responsibilities are allocated?

Kotter and Rathgeber's process includes eight stages – and, crucially, allows room for volunteers and sharing of power, making it particularly suitable for churches:

1 Create a sense of urgency (*not* anxiety – passion and excitement).
2 Build your guiding coalition (or core group).
3 Form strategic vision and initiatives.
4 Enlist volunteer army.
5 Enable action by removing barriers.
6 Generate short-term wins.
7 Sustain acceleration.
8 Institute change.[78]

This model is designed to be sustainable. Ideally, it creates an organization that can then respond well to further changes down the road. It also can incorporate some of the elements of other models we've looked at. Here's an example of how it might work:

1 Create a sense of urgency: think of the ADKAR principles here – first, awareness of the problem, and then desire to change.
2 Build your guiding coalition: is this the PCC? A working group? Look at the material earlier in this book about making a working group as diverse as possible in their points of view. Include community groups if appropriate, and parents

---

78 Kotter, John and Rathgeber, Holger, *That's Not How We Do It Here! A Story About How Organizations Rise and Fall – and Can Rise Again.* London: Penguin Random House, 2016, p. 151.

and, ideally, children and young people themselves. Ensure your meetings are designed so that decision-making isn't predetermined by groupthink.

3 Form strategic vision and initiatives. What do we want our church to look like? How do we get there? This may be when you use the audit tool from Chapter 2.

4 Enlist volunteer army. Again, this may require looking at how people's time is allocated and deciding to end or reconfigure some existing work. This may be a time when the 'ending, losing and letting go' material may be useful.

5 Enable action by removing barriers: this may mean barriers in your building, addressing skills gaps in your clergy, staff and volunteers, addressing toxic church politics (as mentioned in Chapter 2) or knocking down the false assumptions listed in Chapter 4.

6 Generate short-term wins, such as adding a specific and re-assuring welcome to parents and carers at the start of the service, creating a clearly signposted 'buggy park', adding a revived and spiritually imaginative children's corner, routinely reminding the congregation to offer a smile and a helping hand to parents … the simple things that make a difference and get you started and create momentum. This is also the time for experimenting and playing around. What works? What doesn't? Let's try new things. No idea is too crazy, as long as you're willing to try and make it work. It's important that short-term wins are celebrated and recognized by leaders.

7 Sustain acceleration. What needs to be done so that what you're doing can last, without burning everyone out? And what new initiatives need to happen in order to keep the progress going?

8 Institute change. At this point, Kotter and Rathgeber say, 'big wins are institutionalized in the hierarchical structure.' Things that are working well become tradition – the leaders

realize they're working well and want to sustain them, and the volunteers are happy to have what they're doing supported by the 'powers that be'.

Crucially, there is room in this model both for boiling frogs and for shock and awe. Having a strategic vision, and a guiding group, means that change can be made slowly and with consensus – but having a volunteer army given freedom to try new things and see what works allows room for creativity, for responding to external changes (like new housing built in your parish), for quick 'shock and awe' changes, and for the Holy Spirit to lead your church into surprising new places.

But regardless of where you move slowly and where you make dramatic changes, you will hopefully reach a point at which you are making visible changes by including children more in worship.

Participation in worship can take many forms, not just reading a lesson or prayer. Children can join the greeting team or the music team, work on the sound system, make and/or serve refreshments, create drawings or photography for use in the service sheet or slides, create prayer stations, write the prayers, and more.

This may be a big change for the children, and for the rest of the congregation – and it picks up multiple strands from what we've examined so far; assumptions of who church is for, the role children play, whether church is education, entertainment or enculturation, and so on. So you will probably need to take your congregation on a journey of change in how they relate to the growing role of children as leaders and ministers in worship.

If it's all going well, the next step that often happens in the church's journey, past 'Oh, I guess that isn't so bad', is to treat the children's involvement as a performance:

> 'Good job playing the piano in church!'
> 'You read so well!'
> 'You performed the drama so perfectly! You remembered all your lines!'

You're walking a difficult tightrope here, because you want the children to receive positive feedback on their inclusion and you want to show the congregation you're glad they're responding well.

But you also don't want to run the risk of making church a place to perform, where 'how well you read' is more important than the fact that what you're reading is Holy Scripture. I regularly remind children, when we're rehearsing to lead part of worship, that it's worship, not a show. We are not performing for the people in the pews – we're helping them to worship God. God, not the congregation, is who we are giving our worship to, and he will accept it because it comes in love. We want to read clearly and loudly so that people will understand what we're praying for, not because we're actors putting on a show.

One father I spoke with told me his daughter had been terrified of public speaking, until the children's worker at her church asked her to go on the reading rota. Because church was full of people she'd known all her life, and both the children's worker and her father emphasized that it was worship and not performance, she was able to practise reading in public in a context that felt safe. Over the years, this dad said, his daughter's confidence in speaking at school and in other contexts grew greater.

And, as 17-year-old Jess points out, having children as worship leaders helps create a more inclusive church community: '[When] the younger kids are the ones doing the prayers and intercessions and readings, it encourages the older generations – the people you wouldn't normally talk to – to watch you and see what you can do. Especially when we do stuff like the Christmas pageant, when we do solos and acting and dancing or reading or whatever, it's nice for them to be able to see the younger generation enjoying being part of the community.'

Ten-year-old Wren agrees – having jobs to do helps you feel you belong: 'If you've got something to do, you feel, this is nice, I'm happy to be here, or if you're serving, like you're a part of the service.'[79]

If the changes you're making are within what that older generation would still recognize as 'basically still the church I know and love', they will be much more receptive to seeing it as a gift instead of an intrusion. And the younger generation will become enculturated into the ways of being and doing that your community values.

Eventually, if you keep going – pushing the boundaries a little, but staying roughly within your tradition and being honest when something isn't working – you will hopefully pass the 'This wasn't so bad' phase and 'The children performed so

---

79 This may be another tightrope you end up walking – especially if you minister in an area of high academic pressure. Your children will hit stressful points in their lives, like SATS and other exam times, and 'having a job to do' at church may become something else to have to rally their limited energy for, and stress about performing well at. Make sure they know having jobs is an option, but if all they can manage to do is show up ten minutes late in leggings and a dirty hoodie and sit in the back, because they've been revising for GCSEs and their Grade 8 piano exam until 3 a.m., that's also fine.

well!' phase and enter the Promised Land of the 'Wow, what the children presented actually enhanced *my* worship. I learned from them. I saw God in a new way through them' phase.

At the church where I was the children's worker we added an interactive element to our Mothering Sunday prayers. I suggested the children write or draw on paper hearts, something to represent all the people who were like a mum to them. We would then hang these hearts on a tree and bless the tree.

The vicar suggested we have the whole congregation do it, not just the children. So we tried it. Now, older people often tell me after the service, with tears in their eyes, how much it means to them to honour mothers, godmothers, nannies and others who may have died 50 years ago. To name them and see them blessed.

I was completely bowled over. I think they were too. This was something we'd designed for children and it ended up moving adults to tears. Trinity Church has several similar examples – including when adults asked 'Can I have some chalk too?' when children had been sent home with chalk to bless their doors at Epiphany.

This is what happens when you take children seriously as people and as disciples. Children are not a different species from the rest of us, and if you nourish their spirituality you will find that you are inadvertently nourishing the adults' as well. And you are truly becoming an intergenerational community that welcomes all.

### The evolution of attitudes to children leading worship

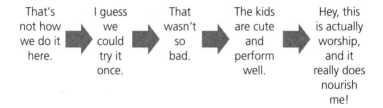

| That's not how we do it here. | I guess we could try it once. | That wasn't so bad. | The kids are cute and perform well. | Hey, this is actually worship, and it really does nourish me! |

Obviously, not 100% of the people in your church will come to that final realization. But if enough of them do, you have the critical mass to shift your culture towards one that sees children as fellow disciples, and even as ministers. You will have people among you who see the presence of children, and a church that welcomes and nourishes them, and gives them opportunities for leadership, not just as something we have to tolerate because we know it's good for the community's future but as something that is valuable to *me, right now.*

There are, however, times when you should ignore everything I've just said about caution and collaboration. The change-management approaches I've discussed are intended to be as collaborative as possible. Ideally, churches that are the unified Body of Christ value everyone – we don't set up an 'us vs them', 'children vs adults' mentality, draw our battle lines and shout 'My way or the highway'. We prefer, when possible, to be broad and inclusive, and not play zero-sum games.

On the other hand, this is the real world, and that's not always possible.

So what are some situations in which a more direct, less 'softly softly' approach might need to be taken? When can you say 'We're going to *do* X' instead of 'We're going to *try* X', act almost unilaterally and go for shock and awe as your default?

- When 'a collaborative approach' has been tried, and it turns out that in practice it means, 'Bullies have a big microphone, and total veto power over everything we're doing, and are not operating in good faith. If we try to appease them, and not move forward too dramatically until they're on board, we'll be here for ever. And the more vulnerable people – the children – have to sit here and just take what the powerful bullies are dishing out, for the sake of unity and collaboration.' That is not okay. And I can't tell you where this line falls in your congregation and your process, because it's different for everyone. It's something you'll have to watch out for and be aware of. As my spiritual director says, 'Do no harm. But take no crap.'[80]
- When you're at serious crisis point. If you're a year away from closure or bankruptcy, and dramatic change is needed, then you don't have the luxury of time and of taking the slowly, slowly approach. You need to make big changes, quickly, to show that the church is serious about saving itself.
- When your community is in a rut, people are bored, uninspired and demoralized, and a big dramatic change from someone bringing in crazy new ideas might be needed to get people excited and enthusiastic again.

---

80 She uses a stronger word than 'crap'.

## Darren's fifth mistake: dropped in and left: 'It's only one Sunday'

Ultimately, Darren wasn't really trying to change Adam's church here. He was trying to do his thing and then leave, leaving Adam to pick up the pieces. Darren's focus is, primarily, on himself, and not on the good of the church he's visiting.

For those of us who are working with our own churches and not just dropping into someone else's, the process of embedding changes is crucial. We can't just put up some fairy lights and beanbags, leave and trust that everything will work out. This means that it can't all depend on one person – if that one person gets hit by a bus and spends six weeks in hospital, the church will revert to the way it was before. And if that person is the vicar, or the children's worker, if they move on to a different post, the church will revert to the way it was before. Culture change is not the same as a cult of personality, or one very talented practitioner. It can't all be on one person's shoulders. It is the work of community. Planning a legacy, and a team, needs to be built into the project from the start.

And part of embedding change is looking at the structures and systems of your church – how decisions are made, by whom, who is invited to meetings, who is represented on which bodies and working groups, how your Mission Action Plan is developed, and so on – and making changes there. We'll look more at this later.

In the next chapter we'll explore a bit about how to truly welcome children and families over the long term – what it means to welcome the whole child and how to welcome them in ways that fully honour them as a beloved child of God and a full member of the Body of Christ.

## Broken Bodies

Sometimes reconciliation is not possible. Change is scary and hard.

One vicar I spoke with had led a very collaborative, pastorally sensitive, open, gentle process of change in their parish, to be more welcoming towards children – and still found that some people couldn't get on board either with the goal or with the process:

> 'The people who found it most difficult had a particular life experience in common. And it took me longer than it should have done to figure out why these things were particularly hard for them. And when I did, I was able to repair bridges with one of them very well, and the other one not so much.
>
> 'People are often deeply deeply damaged and hurt, and some kinds of change and some kinds of process might just be too hard. But that's why you do Communions, Evensong, really nice 8 a.m. services that the vicar does themselves, and why you have a balance in parish life that doesn't make some people unwelcome at the expense of welcoming others. We don't always get that right, but there's a lot we can do – if the church is changing all around them, there are things we can do relationally to make that easier for people. But some people are incredibly broken, and sometimes the thing you do reveals that brokenness in a way you just never knew was there.'

And so this chapter ends where it began – with prayer. The sort of situation described above can be one of the more difficult elements of church leadership – and it can happen to clergy, to children's workers and to volunteers alike. Praying on your own, and with your core group, can help remind you why you're doing this, centre and strengthen you, and help you see where you might have made mistakes and what you can do about them. Praying for the people who are struggling with change can give you perspective on their behaviour and your choices for how you respond to it.

In addition to prayer, there is the need to support. This is another area where having a core group can be helpful – you are not struggling through this process alone. The core group may be able to turn your tears of frustration into laughter, or help you see a solution you wouldn't have thought of on your own. But you also may find you need more support outside your own church – from family, diocesan or other church structures, a spiritual director or counsellor, or simply an activity that reminds you that you are more than a church leader and there is more to your life than this process of change. Rest, retreat, supervision and time away are crucial for any church leader at any time, but especially during times of change. Change is hard work, and you can't pour from an empty cup.

## Discussion Questions

1  Which ideas about change management really resonated with you? Which struck you as 'No, that's not us'?

2  How will you begin the process of forming and communicating a vision for what your church can be in regard to welcoming children and families? A whole-church meeting? Forming a core group? Something else?

3 How will people have an opportunity, as changes are made, to communicate their thoughts and emotions – both positive and negative – to each other and church leaders? What is the role of the core group/working group/PCC/governing body in this?

4 What are the places where a 'boiling frogs' approach might be better, and what are the places where 'shock and awe' might be better?

5 How will you honour and acknowledge the history of the church and what has gone before, without getting stuck there?

6 Whose role might be changing? How will you ensure these people are still given an opportunity to use their gifts and talents towards the service of God in your church?

7 How will the leadership and/or core group look after their own well-being, and maintain boundaries, throughout the process? Who can they turn to for support?

# 6

# Do Not Hinder Them

We have talked earlier about the difference between education, entertainment and worship. Any church that is truly welcoming to children needs to welcome children – not just cheerlead them through repeated renditions of universally happy and cheerful songs and activities but nurture their spirituality, give them stories, prayers, music and worship that takes them seriously, form real relationships with them and include them in making decisions that affect them.

## Take Them Seriously

If children are at church not just to be educated or entertained but to worship God and be enculturated, through community, into what it means to be a Christian, then that has implications on how we use worship and children's groups to make them – the spiritual them – truly welcome.

Welcoming children in church means accepting they are not there just to:

- Hold up pictures of things;
- Be cute for adult approval;
- Receive a simple moral lesson and repeat it back to the adults.

And welcoming children in church means acknowledging that life and the Gospel are not just about bunny rabbits, rainbows and unicorns but about so much more – guilt, loss, terror, exile, homecoming, redemption, pain, family breakdown, broken promises, love, sorrow and, ultimately, death and resurrection.

We may hesitate to expose children to some of these stories. I regularly hear 'Should children come to church on Ash Wednesday/Good Friday/for a funeral?' from well-intentioned, anxious parents or church leaders. As if children would have no concept of sin, or death, if we didn't tell them. We may wish this were true – that children are wholly innocent and pure, but unfortunately it isn't. I worked with a group of children once on putting together a Confession and Absolution for an act of worship. We designed one mural to show the world the way God wants it to be, and another showing the world the way it is. They were deeply aware of environmental destruction, human cruelty and the reality of death.[81]

If we present to children a sanitized Christianity that is entirely free of sin and death, we are selling both children and Christianity short.

We are selling children short because we are failing to give them a place where they can safely explore these difficult and scary concepts. We are showing them that their fear of the world's brokenness and of death is so terrifying that even the adults won't touch it. We are leaving them alone with it. And we are failing to give them the message that faith is big enough and important enough to absorb these concepts.

---

81 There were *lots* of images of pet gravestones in the mural. The death of a pet is often a child's first experience with death, and can be a profound life experience.

We are selling Christianity short because we are taking from it the very source of its power – that the world's brokenness is not God's will, that God's love is stronger than death and that God has fought death for us and won, and given us all a pathway to follow to a life that never ends, in a place where sin is no more. If you cut that message out of the gospel, you cut out its very heart. You make it a lifeless, anaemic thing, good only for cheap grace and trite morality, when what it has to offer is so much more. As G. K. Chesterton said, 'Fairy tales do not tell children the dragons exist. Children already know that dragons exist. Fairy tales tell children the dragons can be killed.' You can replace 'Christianity' for 'fairy tales' here, and 'sin and death' for 'dragons'.

And when we make the Bible simple and sanitized, we cut our children off from the hope given by God's constant use of imperfect people. Moses was a murderer. Joseph was an arrogant so-and-so who, I am sometimes tempted to believe, almost deserved what he got from his brothers. Jacob and Esau's sibling rivalry led to decades of estrangement. Let's not even get started on King David. And Jesus' own disciples were usually jealous, petty, disloyal, squabbling among themselves, and completely missing the point.[82] If we present God's people as perfect, we teach children that they, in their imperfection, mistakes and bad choices, can't be God's people. I am personally reassured by Peter's continual inability to think before he speaks and God's use of him anyway. It suggests there's a place in the Kingdom for me too.

Welcoming children to church means taking them seriously as fellow human beings who are aware that the world is a broken

---

82 I will say nothing about how some PCCs may resemble the disciples …

place, that all living things die and that our lives are often far from what we'd like them to be. Children are not permanently happy innocent people whose spirituality is nourished by being cheerled through a bunch of songs about how happy we always feel because of Jesus, followed by a Bible story told out of context and distilled into a simplistic moral lesson (usually about being good, listening to the adults or sharing). God is so much more than that, and children are so much more than that.

To be truly welcoming of children, in all that they are and all that they experience, we need to take their capacity for awe and wonder seriously (as well as their humour, silliness and need to move around), and invite them into a place where they can safely explore the big questions of life, death, loss and redemption. We need to offer them rich, nourishing storytelling, music, reflection and prayer. Some books that explore children's spirituality further are in the Resource List at the end of this book.

# Form Real Relationships With Them

If taking children seriously means creating opportunities for them to foster their relationship with God, this section is about fostering relationships with each other and with adults who aren't their parents.[83]

I interviewed some children and young people from my own church and asked them what helps them feel welcome in a new

---

83 Obligatory footnote to say that Safeguarding is the necessary first step here, and that it's not just a box-ticking exercise but absolutely crucial to the impressions children form about church, about Christians and, most importantly, about God.

place. What makes you feel like you belong? What gets in the way?

I expected to hear a variety of answers about 'knowing how you're supposed to behave' or 'knowing what to expect and how things work', but their answers almost uniformly focused on building relationships.

Wren, aged ten, said, 'To make me not feel welcome, if people go round in one group on purpose.' That feeling of cliquishness can become an almost invisible and ingrained part of our churches' cultures – especially if we haven't had many new people for a while and everyone already knows each other. Being the new person in that situation is very difficult, especially if you're also a different age from everyone else.

Mary, aged 16, agreed: 'People ignoring you, making no effort to get to know you or understand you or get your sense of humour or where you're coming from can make you feel unwelcome', whereas, 'When people welcome you warmly, they acknowledge that you don't really know people, and they make an effort to get to know you. When they acknowledge your presence, it makes you feel more welcome and appreciated.'

When I asked them what could be done to make this happen, Delilah, who is 12, said, 'Sunday school. Because little children find it easier to socialize with each other. You need to have Sunday school so, like, when you go up to Sunday school and you make bread, that kind of makes you speak to other people and be friends with other people. Having Sunday school definitely makes you feel together.'

Much of the recent thinking on children in church encourages intergenerationality and suggests that children feel excluded when they spend time in Junior Church or separate groups. For Delilah, however, some time spent just with other children was important – it helped her bond and make friends.

However, I quoted Delilah's sister Jess in the Introduction and for her, spending time with older people was an important part of church: 'There's something about older people that I really like. I think they're wise. There's something about security, around older people, that I really love.'

And Sam Richards points out that if children only ever meet people their own age at church, 'Moving up [from one programme to another] means starting again with no prior understanding of what it might mean to be a 12/18/25/45/65-year-old Christian, and how that generational group might relate together.'[84] So it may be that a 'mixed economy' helps children foster real relationships with others in church – some time spent just with children, some time with the whole community.

Matilda, who is 14, said it's important to have that time 'after church, when everyone goes downstairs and talks with each other and has coffee'. Our church also has a balcony, away from the coffee space, where our children have been playing a game of 'dodge-pillow' that's lasted approximately ten years so far. Usually, kids spend that time running back and forth between the main social area, chatting with adults, and the balcony, playing noisily with each other. We may not think of the coffee time as hugely important – it's almost routine – but for children, that time is crucial for their sense of feeling welcome. (And if there's nothing for children – no biscuits or juice – they will not feel welcomed or included in that time.)

---

84 Richards, Sam, 'Family Picnic', in *Re-thinking Children's Work in Churches: A Practical Guide*, London: Jessica Kingsley Publishers, 2019, p. 138.

At a training day on All-Age Worship, the Revd Mary Hawes and the Revd Ally Barrett reminded us that worship takes place within the context of church. And if there are opportunities for children and families to build relationships in the life and work of the church outside Sunday morning, that will pay off in worship. 'It's harder', they said, 'to tut at a child you know.'

Most churches do have opportunities for fellowship outside Sunday morning. As Delilah pointed out, 'The other stuff the church does – like, the announcement today about the singing thing in a few days, and the Christian Aid quiz night and stuff. You're not specifically invited to it, but you know that if you want to come, you can come. And that makes you feel welcome because you can go if you want to but you don't have to go.'

But do children know they can come to these things? There's no reason children can't come to a scratch choir event or a quiz night – do you say so, when you announce these events? Are they held at times that would be compatible with school and a relatively sensible bedtime? Or is everything held at lunchtime on a weekday? Could you provide childcare for very small kids, so parents could come to your quiz night without needing to hire a babysitter? Things like pancake parties, carolling, charity bake sales and so on are easy ways to include all generations in the broader life of the church and create opportunities for relationships to develop outside Sunday morning.

Not all of this has to be provided by your specific church. Joining in with things happening in your deanery or diocese, even with only a few children, can pay dividends in helping them feel welcome and form stronger bonds that will keep them coming back. 'Especially when we're older,' 16-year-old Mary said, 'doing things like the diocesan youth weekend and the homelessness sleepout. I went in only seeing a few of the people from church once a week, and not all the time, and then we spent two consecutive days together, travelling, sharing a room – and it was nice getting to understand new things about people and about their lives.'

If you have a regular series of things outside Sunday morning (even if it's only a few events a year), which you can invite families and children to, you have a pathway for them to begin to feel like they belong, they're welcome and they know people at your church. They can then be comfortable turning up on Sunday morning without feeling completely alien, out of place and scared of being judged.

If you don't have personal or professional experience with children with additional needs, or with traumatic backgrounds that can lead to behavioural challenges, you may find it more difficult to form relationships with them. Again, remember that children know themselves. Parents and carers know their children. The children themselves, and those who care for them, are the first experts to consult if you need help in figuring out what works for them. But keeping the following in mind can help:

1  Poverty means insecurity. Ensuring there is always 'enough and more than enough' – of art supplies, of time and attention, of biscuits after the service – can help reassure children that church is a safe place.
2  If you are in a position of authority, find training on positive discipline that helps you reward constructive behaviour and address negative behaviour without criticizing the child ('You need to change your behaviour' rather than 'You're being bad').

3 Consistency, routine and clear expectations matter – especially to children on the autism spectrum and those whose home lives may be chaotic and unpredictable.

4 Notice children being good. And make sure your definition of being good isn't just 'doing what the adults say' but helping each other, waiting their turn, sharing and so on.

5 Provide spaces where children who need to take time apart from the group can do so safely. A chill-out zone may help a child with autism when they have sensory overload, or may help a child struggling with their behaviour to gather their emotions together before returning to the group.

6 Any sudden negative changes in a child's behaviour may indicate a safeguarding concern.

7 When correcting behaviour, provide an alternative. Don't just say 'Stop running – the service is about to start', say 'Can you help me hand out these service sheets to everyone coming in?'

8 Understand that each child is an individual. Have a realistic grasp of different ages and different additional needs. Celebrate every child's gifts and development, as well as the milestones that matter to them. Have expectations that are both realistically high and generous. Try, where possible, to recognize the difference between a child who is genuinely doing their best but may have challenges, and one deliberately trying to get a rise out of you or disrupt things (again, parents and carers can help here). Give children what they need for them to participate in their own way, and celebrate what they can do and who they are. Remember that every single child shows us something about God by being who they are.

And in forming relationships with children, it's important to remember that when they are very young, making space for relationships with children means making space for relationships with parents.

I was once standing with several baptism families who had come back for our Harvest Festival. They all had babies or young toddlers. A new family walked in who had never been to our church before, but who knew a few of the families I was standing with. One mum gestured her friend over, introduced her to all of us and said, 'This is a great church. There are lots of people here who will hold the baby if you need to pee.'

As a practical, relatable sign of welcome for young families, that struck me as one of the greatest compliments anyone has ever paid our community. It's a sign of extra pairs of hands, belonging to people you know and trust, and who will help you carry the load of raising your child in the church.

We may believe that the parents in our community, especially those whose children we've baptized, already know that we're like this. And that if they wanted to come, they would. But vicar and mum Lydia says, 'I spoke with my PCC about making a statement on our website about our welcome to families. They asked why we would need to do that, because people already *knew* how welcoming the church was! There was no need to say so explicitly! And anybody who did want to come to church probably already came to church or was a friend of somebody who came to church and could ask them. And the idea that the church might need to say something official about how it feels about particular things was completely outside their experience – they didn't see a need for it to communicate in that way.'

Lydia is right. Very often parents *don't* know they're welcome. Church is relatively unfamiliar to them. They're worried about their children's behaviour. They don't know if you'll welcome or help them – if you'll hold the baby when they need to pee. So tell them. Invite them, over and over. Reassure them. Communicate with them. Build that relationship with them. Let them know they're wanted and valued. And remind your congregation to give them a smile, a word of reassurance and a helping hand when they're trying to juggle a four-year-old, a newborn and a hymnal, all at once. Because they need to know that we think what they're doing – bringing their children into the heart of the Body of Christ, to encounter God through the apostles' teaching and fellowship, the breaking of the bread and the prayers – is important and wonderful.

## Include Them in Making Decisions That Affect Them

Earlier, I put forward a few different images of childhood – the blank slate, the seedling, the fellow pilgrim. The fellow pilgrim is the one that most closely aligns with much of what's going on in other areas of the child's life – school, council services, the family court system and more. In religious language, we may call this 'acknowledging the child as a full disciple of Christ and a full member of the Body of Christ, as they are now, not because of their future potential'. In civic language, this image of childhood views the child as a citizen, with rights.

The most formal expression of this view of childhood was set down in 1989 in the UN Convention on the Rights of the Child, to which the UK is a signatory. And Scripture, as discussed in Chapter 4, views children as complete human beings, capable of prophecy and leadership. Jesus held them up as examples and role models, and they were key to some of his miracles.

So a church culture that truly values children, that holds a scriptural view of them, is one that should take a rights-based approach to welcoming children seriously. Ruth Radley, of the Church Mission Society, regularly works with communities in South Sudan to develop models of the rights-based approach to children in community. She writes, 'The Church should not be playing catch-up with the so-called "secular" world ... belatedly but increasingly allowing [children] to participate, ensuring that their voices are heard, enabling them to develop as God intended to. Rather, the Church should be out in the front, fearlessly leading the way in speaking out about children's rights, AND their responsibilities, as well as the responsibilities of their caregivers and the wider community.'[85]

The rights-based approach is a cultural challenge to our churches. The UN Convention itself makes challenging reading if we compare it to how our churches function.[86] Article 3 states, 'The best interests of the child must be a top priority in all decisions and actions that affect children', while Article 12 says that 'Every child has the right to express their views, feelings and wishes in all matters affecting them, and to have their views considered and taken seriously.'

If our churches are to develop a culture that truly welcomes children, surely these are the sorts of goals we should be aspiring to – the child not just as a blank slate or a seedling but as a human being equal to ourselves. But, the Convention points out, children are not just fellow citizens (or in religious terms,

---

85 Radley, Ruth, 'Superhero, Advocate, and Idol', in *Re-thinking Children's Work in Churches: A Practical Guide*, London: Jessica Kingsley Publishers, 2019, p. 152.

86 You can read the Convention, or a summary of it, at www.unicef.org.uk/what-we-do/un-convention-child-rights/.

fellow disciples). They are also in need of special protections because of their vulnerability.

The rights-based approach acknowledges children as equal citizens with adults (Gal. 3.28: 'There is no longer Jew or Greek, there is no longer slave or free, there is no longer male and female') while also acknowledging that for various reasons, they are more vulnerable and in need of protection (Matt. 25.40; 18.6: 'just as you did it to one of the least of these … you did it to me' / 'If any of you put a stumbling-block before one of these little ones who believe in me, it would be better for you if a great millstone were fastened around your neck and you were drowned in the depth of the sea.').

Children cannot vote. In our churches, they cannot serve on the PCC until they're 16. They're not even counted on the electoral role until that age – they're virtually invisible. And yet almost every decision made by the adults will affect them.

So the rights-based approach challenges us to ask the questions: Who holds the power? Who makes decisions about, and for, children? Who decides who belongs and who participates?

Sometimes, these big questions lead to surprisingly practical and simple changes. The Revd Ally Barrett told me:

'After I left frontline vicaring and we moved to a new city, I asked my children how many churches they thought there were in our new city, as we were driving past a few. I asked, "How do you know that you belong to ours? It's not our parish church. How do you know you belong there?"

'And my son said, "You know you belong when you're on a rota, because when you're on a rota it shows they know your name, and when they know your name, it means they've noticed you and you matter and they'd miss you if you weren't there." Which I thought was a pretty profound summary of empowered children, but also how rotas and those things work – we tend to think of them as administrative, but they're actually massively symbolic.'

Who's in charge of your rota? Who decides who to ask? Do people – including children – have the opportunity to speak up and say they'd like to be considered for jobs, or is your culture of participation one of 'Wait to be asked'?

I asked Ally how to open up the rota:

'Every Lent, we used to put up lists of all the rotas that people could be on. And all the committees, with the list of names of people who were already doing them. And the idea was that you could take Lent to work out if you wanted to carry on doing the same thing, or if you wanted to do a new thing, and you knew who to ask if you wanted to try it. It was a great system, and it was in time for the APCM …

'The Lent after we had our first All-Age Eucharist – I put the list up as usual and all the kids, without any prompting at all, signed up on rotas. Because, I think, they'd realized that they were fully members of the church.'

Being on a rota also marks one crucial transition in being part of a community – going from 'service recipient' to 'part of the community'. When you have a job to do, you're not just going to church to receive something, you are participating in making it. You are part of the community, and it goes both ways.

Ally says the rota is one area where something 'can be converted from stumbling block to cornerstone'. 'Rotas', she says, 'are often among the most strongly gatekept things in the church, and they will be the domain of particular people, and so the way that the church does its rotas can speak volumes about how in you are. That's not just about kids, that's about newcomers, that's about people who don't quite fit, a whole bunch of reasons people might find the rota thing a bit of an in-crowd experience, something that makes them feel not quite welcome. You don't want to overwhelm people by making them join something right away, but having some kind of system where people feel that they can volunteer for things and will be accepted, and that they might be invited to become stakeholders and have some agency as well as just recipients.'

At their weekly family service, St Albans Church in Teddington has a 'rota that isn't a rota'. Every job that needs doing is out on a table, as a laminated card – when people of any age arrive, if they want to do a job, they take the card for that job. This is an open, democratic system, with a minimum of administrative fuss, and no hidden gatekeeper. You can ring the bell, light the candles or take up the collection no matter what age you are, whether this is your first time at church or your 1,000th.

Sharing power is an enormous part of cultural change. I've seen this first hand in my own ministry, even in very small ways – I use Godly Play 'I wonder ...' questions after we tell Bible stories, such as 'I wonder what the most important part of this story is.' I've also used this occasionally in All-Age Worship, as part of a sermon.

One important principle of wondering questions is that there's no right or wrong answer. Children and adults alike find this disconcerting at first. I've seen parents lean over to whisper the 'right answer' in their child's ear and make them put their hand up to say it. The child who is used to getting the 'right answer' in class may confidently go first and then be surprised when I say, 'Thank you – any other thoughts?' and take someone else's idea too. Adults who are used to having Scripture interpreted *for* them by the preacher may hesitate to speak up. 'I wonder …' questions are open, they level the playing field of power and they offer anyone who wants to the chance to meaningfully participate in interpreting Scripture.

In some churches, the problem may be convincing the leadership to open that power up to the congregation, especially children. But in others, it may be the opposite. At a conference, a friend and I were listening to a speaker talk passionately about how church leaders needed to learn to stop clinging to power, and share the decision-making. My friend leaned over to me and said, 'I *wish* my congregation would let me share power with them!'

In some places – I would imagine in pastoral-size and programme-size churches – the cultural attitude of 'We put money in the collection plate so the vicar will do X for us and we don't have to' prevails. Part of creating a cultural change that has room for children to participate in decision-making, be taken seriously as theologians and included in the systems and structures of the church may be training both children and adults in new ways of taking responsibility for their own spiritual journey.

Kate, a vicar in the north of England, talks about a journey she took with some adults as part of preparing her church to be more welcoming to children. 'I found a Lent course about religious poetry', she says. 'At the start, I found I had to do a lot of the input. [My congregation] had never been empowered to have opinions about poetry or ask questions about it. Good art is open questions, but nobody had allowed them to know that.'

By the end of the course, however, things had changed. 'After doing this week by week – and it helped that there were excellent lunches, and that hospitality kind of leaked into the discussions – they were really enjoying themselves. I could put poems in front of them and just get them going and they would run with it, and they were starting to ask questions, share ideas, disagree with other – which was fantastic.'

Kate modelled a more democratic way of doing theology, and this helped her congregation realize they had power. 'I honestly think,' Kate said, 'without that process of being freed up a little bit and to eat together, I'm not sure we could have had the All-Age Eucharist. So I think the poetry stuff really prepared the ground – because this was a lot of the older members of the church, who were perhaps most resistant to changing the worship.' By realizing there was a different way of doing things, where power resided with the congregation, and where open questions, disagreement and *play* were valued, they became more ready to welcome children.

Because what Kate was doing, in helping them respond to open questions, disagreement and play, was helping them become more like children themselves. And when we are more child-like, we're more open to the presence of children. 'I was trying', she says, 'to liberate them into daring to do things and interact in ways that had perhaps been taught out of them. I think a lot of adults have been quite oppressed by their education. And a lot of people in my parish have been taught that poetry, and art, and so on, was for people of a higher class and it wasn't for them, or that they don't understand that and shouldn't talk about it.

And if we all had that attitude towards theology, nobody would ever do any of it.'

Where are the opportunities in your church to teach adults about being playful, and encourage them to take control over their own spiritual journeys? Dean Pusey, a former diocesan youth officer, regularly says that a church cannot disciple its young people if it doesn't disciple its adults – you need significant adults within the church community to be part of the village that welcomes, and nurtures, the child and young person in their spiritual journey. Teaching adults to play, to talk about faith and to not cede everything at church to the leadership is ultimately crucial in providing a place of welcome that will truly nurture children as disciples of Jesus.

Children may even be more used to this way of working than adults are. Changes in the prevailing culture of schools over the last 25 or 50 years have meant that children may be used to disagreeing, open questions and participation in decision-making than adults are. The Revd Dr Nigel Genders, the chief education officer of the Church of England, wrote that worship in schools is 'participatory and engaging. Children are encouraged to be leaders of as well as participants in worship.'[87] In wider school culture, children are now routinely 'actively enabled to contribute towards the functioning of the school community. It started with school councils, but it is now commonplace for children to also be involved in interviewing teachers and school leaders, driving initiatives such as charitable activity and community service, and engaging in peer-to-peer mentoring.'[88]

---

87 Genders, Nigel, 'Education and Mission: Schools, Churches and Families, A Discussion Paper', presented to the House of Bishops for consultation, Epiphany 2018.
88 Ibid.

However, often, children find that this culture of participation and decision-making is not reflected at church. 'Anecdotally,' Genders says, 'young people tell us that they are not often involved in decision-making or given leadership responsibility in the church. When the Church talks of setting God's people free, or of growing leadership or reimagining ministry, it is often interpreted as being adult focused, rather than recognizing that children and young people should be active participants in these areas.' Research done in 2016 supports this – the *Rooted in the Church* report interviewed young people who stayed in church, in order to establish what worked for them. It found that: 'Young people seek to be treated as equal members of the Church. They want to have meaningful roles, not tokenism. This includes leadership roles and serving opportunities, including intergenerational ministry. They also seek a greater "voice and vote" on decision-making bodies such as PCCs and Synods.'[89]

The website 'Learn to Listen' is an excellent resource, with toolkits, session plans and more, on increasing meaningful participation and decision-making from children and young people.[90]

The church where I was the children's worker, like many churches, had our AGM after church one Sunday in April, and a DVD was available in a separate room for children. One year, a group of children (the youngest was about six) decided they'd rather come to the meeting. So I found myself, at this big important church meeting, at a table that, unlike the rest, consisted largely of people aged six to sixteen. (In retrospect, I should have prepared for this and encouraged them to come

---

89 *Rooted in the Church*, p. 7, at www.churchofengland.org/sites/default/files/2017-11/Rooted%20in%20the%20Church%20Summary%20Report.pdf.

90 www.learn-to-listen.org.uk/.

to the meeting. As at so many other times, the children were ahead of me.)

I got marker pens so they could draw and take notes, asked them what they most remembered about church from the last year, encouraged them to raise their hand for the microphone when they had an idea, and helped them brainstorm ideas when the meeting's chair had us work in groups.

Think about where decisions are made and ideas shared in your church – the AGM? Sub-committees on worship, charitable work, mission, stewardship and so on? Is there any way to include children and young people in at least some of these decision-making bodies?[91] Church of England parishes allow young people to join the PCC at age 16 – even if you aren't able to get any teenagers on to your governing body, are there a few children and/or young people who could attend a few meetings a year as ex officio members, to share their perspectives and ideas? If you're appointing a new vicar or children's worker, are children included in the consultation and hiring process?[92]

And if you include children in these decision-making processes, are you willing, where possible, to act on what they say? Because otherwise it's just tokenistic, and they'll know it.

Sherry Arnstein, an American civil servant, formulated a 'ladder of participation' in 1969 to describe her experiences of working

---

91 You may find, as I have, that you end up in a loop. 'Worship is boring. We should change it', a teenager says. 'Okay,' you reply, 'how? I'd love to hear your ideas!' The teenager replies, 'I dunno', and changes the subject. But at least now I'm *asking*. I'm going to call that progress.

92 'Learn to Listen' has session plans specifically for the appointment of a vicar – you can find them at www.learn-to-listen.org.uk/appointing-a-new-vicar/appointing-a-vicar-ways-to-involve-children-and-young-people.

### Models of participation

*i) What many churches look like*

*Here, children's ministry is an afterthought, out by itself, with less time/ money devoted to it than to everything else the church does.*

*ii) A better model*

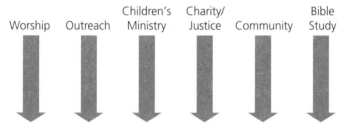

*Here, it is central, considered just as important as everything else and resourced accordingly.*

*iii) An even better model*

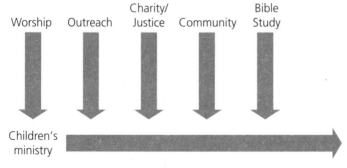

*Here, children are included, and considered, in everything the church is doing.*

with communities in decision-making. This has been developed and adapted in other contexts, and it's highly applicable to children and church. The sociologist Roger Hart specifically adapted it to work with young people and adults in 1997.

RUNG ONE: Young people are manipulated.
RUNG TWO: Young people are decoration.
RUNG THREE: Young people are tokenized.
RUNG FOUR: Young people are assigned tasks and informed of them.
RUNG FIVE: Young people are consulted, and informed of result.
RUNG SIX: Actions are adult-initiated, with decisions shared between adults and young people.
RUNG SEVEN: Young people lead and initiate action.
RUNG EIGHT: Young people and adults share decision-making.

The bottom three rungs, Hart agued, are not genuine participation. At these levels, according to Arnstein, those without power – in this case, children – are being nominally included, but the goal is to get them to go along with the status quo, accepting the decisions of those already in power.

In the middle, children are being told about what's going on, and their views are being sought. This is an enormous positive step forward. However, power still resides with those who originally held it. The powerful (adults) can choose to ignore the opinions of the children, and there's nothing anyone can do about it. The status quo can easily remain.

After this, you reach a level of partnership. Of course, decisions still sometimes need to be made that contradict the desires of children – nobody is saying to let children eat 38 Easter eggs in a row during Sunday worship. But systems and structures can still be arranged to give children and young people meaningful decision-making powers, in areas of genuine importance. In any system where the ladder of participation is used to address power imbalances between groups, 'the underlying issues are essentially the same – "nobodies" … are trying to become "somebodies" with enough power to make the target institutions responsive to their views, aspirations, and needs.'[93] Children deserve to be 'somebodies' in our churches.

The process of changing your culture may take a while. There may be times when it feels like two steps forward, one step (or more) back. But slowly and surely – maybe with the occasional moment of 'shock and awe' to get people to see a new way – you've found that the church that used to be insular, uncertain about children and occasionally outright hostile to parents has turned into a place that sees children as a gift, welcomes them, holds the baby when the parents need both hands, prays for baptism families, knits Nativity scenes for the Pray and Play area, includes children and young people in decision-making and has real and meaningful participation from children in worship, fellowship, teaching and justice work.

How can you maintain this? How can you turn this new way of being into 'the way we've always done it, which nobody would dare change'?

Well, hopefully, you've paid attention to what's been said about using teamwork from the start, so this change is bigger than just one or two people. But you can also make sure you use the systems and structures of your church to embed the changes.

---

93 Arnstein, Sherry R., 'A Ladder of Citizen Participation', *Journal of the American Institute of Planners* 35:4, July 1969, pp. 216–24.

One model of change management I've only mentioned in passing is Kurt Lewin's three-stage model: unfreezing, changing and refreezing. While many of the other models I've looked at focus on the process of initiating and managing change, Lewin looks at how to make that change last. Lewin 'found the refreezing step to be especially important to ensure that people do not revert back to their old ways of thinking or doing prior to the implementation of the change'.[94] He points out the importance of positive rewards and acknowledgement of effort when people display the desired behaviours – positive reinforcement isn't just for children. We all have a tendency to repeat behaviour that's rewarded.

The ADKAR model mentioned in the previous chapter also includes this final stage – Reinforcement is the last step, which is needed to maintain the change.

While often it feels like continual change is the norm, and there's no time to embed new changes, it's worth looking at this step not as setting in a NEW PERFECT WAY OF DOING EVERYTHING, but rather of embedding the changes we have made to our culture so that we are, in general, more open and inclusive, and therefore more able to change as needed in the future.

This means changing structures and systems so that changes in culture can outlast the people who initially led them. It means, as Kotter and Rathgeber put it, that 'big wins are institutionalized in the hierarchical structure'.[95] Things that started as experiments become formal departments, with a boss and staff – or, in church language, with a committee and regular attention in

---

94 From https://study.com/academy/lesson/lewins-3-stage-model-of-change-unfreezing-changing-refreezing.html.

95 Kotter, John and Rathgeber, Holger, *That's Not How We Do It Here! A Story About How Organizations Rise and Fall – and Can Rise Again.* London: Penguin Random House, 2016, p. 155.

PCC meetings. For example, by making it standard that a group of children report to the PCC several times a year, including a few under-16s on your worship committee, and ensuring that their opinions are taken seriously in decision-making, you're not committing yourself to doing things a certain way. You're still flexible and able to change. But what you've embedded in your structures is a way of including children in the decision-making process.

Intergenerational community – with meaningful relationships and participation – is good for everyone. Research has shown that interaction with children has a beneficial effect on the physical and mental health of older people[96] (we saw this for ourselves in the wonderful 2017 Channel 4 programme *Old People's Home For 4 Year Olds*). Parents and carers benefit by breaking out of the isolation of nuclear families and returning to the village model of raising children. Children benefit by having love and care from a community of all ages, models of what it looks like to be different ages, and a community that marks significant rites of passage in their lives with them.

And when that community is a church, there's even more benefit. Older people can have their faith refreshed and inspired by new perspectives from children – as mine is on a regular basis. Children have a communion of saints around them to help enculturate them into what it means to live out their baptismal vows. Parents have support and encouragement for how to raise their children as disciples of Jesus. And when that church is a welcoming, loving, inclusive place, that takes children seriously and values their opinions, that church is doing the amazing work of liberating each child to be exactly who God has created them to be, to help them know God as

---

96 www.bath.ac.uk/case-studies/how-old-peoples-home-for-4-year-olds-might-force-a-shake-up-in-social-care/.

they are known, to take their place in God's story and to claim it as their own. Behind all the committee meetings, the difficult conversations, the audits, the budget decisions – that's what it's about. That is wonderful, amazing work to be doing. And, with help and prayer, you can do it.

## Discussion Questions

1 Where are the opportunities to build relationships between people of all ages in your church?

2 Where are the opportunities for people who are new to build relationships with your existing congregation? Who is good at reaching out and befriending people? (Think of both adults and children here.) How can children get to know each other, and parents get to know the other adults in your church?

3 How can you deliberately make the most of opportunities to stay in touch with families you may meet only occasionally, and make sure they're invited and encouraged to come back? Who can take responsibility for ensuring this is done regularly?

4 Using Lydia's emphasis on the baptismal promises as the starting point – where, in your church, can children 'take their place within the life and worship of Christ's church'? If there is no place, how can you go about starting to make one?

5 How can you include children and young people in the decision-making processes of the church? How can you encourage them to take their role as leaders in worship and in the life of the church, in ways that truly hear their voices?

# Afterword: From Stranger to Friend

## Sandra Millar

### *Head of Welcome and Life Events, The Church of England*

All my life I have been involved in welcoming people. That's because I grew up as a child in the world of retail, and began my working life in the same area. In that world, you learn very quickly that what happens when people walk through your door will have an impact on whether they go away feeling positive, or telling their friends about their negative experiences. And at its best, welcome leads people not just to visit once but to return and become that cherished individual, the loyal customer.

Along with this background, I have also had a long passion for seeing children and young people welcomed, valued and engaged in all aspects of life, and especially in the life of the church. From the day Jesus turned rejection into acceptance when he blessed the children, recorded in all the Gospels, through his transformation of a boy's lunch into a miracle, to his raising of a 12-year-old back to life, the Gospels challenge us to take seriously the idea that children absolutely have a place in God's heart and with God's people.

*Beyond the Children's Corner* connects with all these themes. The book is full of challenges and questions, resources and ideas, all interjected with the reality of experience rooted in parish life. And although much of this relates to welcome for everyone at whatever age and stage we meet them, what is crucial is that we don't lose sight of the longing to see children, young people and their families flourish as they find their role in the household of God's people.

'Welcome' is such a small word for something that goes far beyond opening a door and handing out books. In his book *Reaching Out*, Henri Nouwen writes about the move from hostility to hospitality. Nouwen defines hospitality as creating the space where people can become who God has created them to be.

> Hospitality, therefore, means primarily the creation of a free space where the stranger can enter and become a friend instead of an enemy. Hospitality is not to change people but to offer them space where change can take place.[97]

Interestingly, he then goes on to talk about the child as stranger and how that child can become the unique individual that God created her to be. This understanding gives a much bigger vision to welcome, and it is this big vision that will involve churches in thinking about every aspect of their lives if they truly want to welcome children and families.

The Church of England is losing contact with children and their families every week, and fewer and fewer people are aware of all that we do and offer. Helpfully, this book reminds us that

---

97 Nouwen, Henri, *Reaching Out: The Three Movements of the Spiritual Life*, London: Fount, 1998, p. 49.

the children, young people and families we meet are coming to us from a changing society and culture, sometimes bringing memories of what church might have been in the past, and sometimes with no idea at all of what to expect. An understanding of context, and taking time to do some deep thinking and reading about the world in which those we want to welcome live and move and have their being, is time well spent. In her recent book *Changing Shape*,[98] Ruth Perrin explores how the generation often called 'millennials' (born between 1981 and 1996) understand and experience the world, exploring the cultural change they have lived through and the impact this has on how they now engage with meaning and faith. Recently I have been reflecting on the story of Zacchaeus and am very struck by the fact that Zacchaeus is the one who takes the risk and makes himself vulnerable, subject to ridicule and criticism by those around him, in his desire just to get a glimpse of Jesus. Sometimes, as those familiar with church we forget just how much of a risk those who come to us are taking, and how fearful they may be at whatever age and stage they are in life

The initial moment of welcome, whether at Sunday worship, Christmas Day, a toddler group, a lunch club, wedding, christening or funeral, has a massive impact on what happens next on faith journeys. Margaret has drawn on this – and other research to show how that involves parents as well as children, and how it expands to thoughts about every aspect of church life. However, initial moments are not always first moments: the experience of welcome has to be consistent over several contacts, deepening so that children have a profound sense of belonging. It may be that your church's biggest contact with children and families is at Christmas services, or through special school

---

98 Perrin, Ruth, *Changing Shape: The Faith Lives of Millennials*, London: SCM Press, 2020.

events, and for many the regularity of these events shapes their sense of belonging. For other children, contact with church might come through being present at Mum and Dad's wedding, or through attending the funeral of a much-loved grandparent. Over a couple of years children, young people and their families may have had several such 'first encounters', which for them form the basis of belonging to church.

In 2018 the Life Events team conducted some research with couples with no recent church experience who had to attend at least six times to make a connection so they could be married in their chosen church. Although a small cohort of 200, there was much in this research that made us think about welcome, and reminded us that there will always be people for whom regular Sunday worship is a point of contact. We learned many things from that research, but perhaps one of the most interesting was how quickly people begin to feel that a place is 'their' church. This happens when those at church take an interest in them, and when they begin to take an interest in the life of the church. This is just as applicable to children as it is to adults – taking an interest in their lives, having an awareness of what is current for them is really important. This doesn't mean that we have to become overly familiar with contemporary children's media, whether TV, books or games, but we do need to be people who show an interest in others by starting a conversation and asking the kind of questions that are genuine.

Changing our churches to become places with a culture of welcome that is truly embracing of all ages is something that requires deep thinking and reflection of our own attitudes to children, and more broadly to newcomers, especially those we experience as different from ourselves. The difference may simply be that they are at a stage of life that we are no longer in, or perhaps have never experienced. In one parish where I ministered I was trying to get people to think about whether we could put information about church at either end of the 'cut through' road where the church was located, somewhat out of the way. Someone was brave enough to say in a puzzled voice: 'But why would we want to do that?' Being honest enough to examine leadership attitudes and identify the barriers to change is part of the transformation of culture that is needed. It may also involve being very honest about the resources that we have available and allowing people to step in or step out as needed. Sometimes we fail to realize that the children and families themselves are part of the resource that is needed.

Thinking about welcome in the broadest sense inevitably leads to thinking about access: the ways in which our buildings and premises impact the sense of belonging and inclusion. In their book *The Power of Moments*,[99] Chip and Dan Heath describe an exercise in which church leaders were invited to look around their premises with a different perspective. It dawned on them that although they were host to a large Spanish-speaking congregation, not one notice or signpost was in anything but English. Putting ourselves 'in their shoes' is a great first step to thinking about the problem spaces but also to thinking about the special spaces in our buildings. As welcome moves from being a one-time-at-the-door experience to embrace everything that happens each time a child, young person or their parents enter the space, so we begin to realize how significant the space itself might be. In my book *Worship Together*, I tell the story of a child who when asked what he liked most about church, simply made a huge gesture with his arms to embrace the chancel space, saying 'I like this ... and all of this.' That's often one of the attractions of cathedral space too. I recall a father telling me

---

99 Heath, C. and Heath, D., *The Power of Moments: Why Certain Experiences have Extraordinary Impact*, London: Bantam Press, 2017.

how his memory of being in the biggest space he had ever seen stayed with him all his life.

Attitudes to welcome are also embedded in our use of language – the casual way we say 'everyone' when we don't actually mean children and young people, or haven't embraced them in our thinking. I recall being at a meeting with Bishop Michael Perham, planning a series of services at which 'the baptized' were going to renew their vows and be challenged to think about their discipleship. All the services were scheduled for 8.00 p.m., so eventually I asked which group of 'all the baptized' were in mind – those who were two, three, eight, ten and so on, or just those over 18? We did manage to get one service on a Sunday afternoon. This is about a change of attitude rather than just asking the children to take part, and involves being specific about who we think might respond. One of my favourite films is *Ratatouille*, in which a rat believes the title of a book *Anyone Can Cook*, and takes up a career as a chef. He took the title at face value. He believed that 'anyone' included him. That is the challenge for us as the church – when we say anyone, or every-one, or all, how are we going to respond when people of all ages take us at our word and ask to be involved?

Being involved turns out to be very important. One non-church regular wedding couple talked movingly about being asked to take up the offertory after their third or fourth visit – they couldn't believe they were being asked to do something so clearly special. In contrast, another couple talked about listening to the notices, which included a request for help at the upcoming church fete. Those willing to help were told to offer help to someone after the service. So during coffee the young couple, travelling 80 miles to attend this church, approached the woman and offered to run a bookstall. With the best of intentions the woman replied, 'Oh, but we didn't mean you!'

She didn't want them to feel burdened or put upon, but instead they were seeing themselves as part of the church community – the good news is that they did indeed end up running a bookstall! This kind of assumption is easily made about children as well, whereas being involved and helping can also make a big difference to them.

Since 2015 it has been possible for children to be chalice assistants at communion, and in some church traditions there are opportunities for young people to be servers in different ways, to sing in choirs, be part of music groups, to help with sound, welcome at the door and many other roles. This has to be done intentionally and seriously to avoid it becoming tokenistic: it is not just about an appearance of diversity but a genuine appreciation that children are part of the Body of Christ. This may also lead churches to think carefully about admitting children to communion before confirmation. There is a growing body of experience that shows how inclusion at this stage enables children to feel part of the Body of Christ. When we say the words 'We are all one body because we share one bread' it becomes increasingly uncomfortable to think about those who are not sharing bread simply on the basis of their years. There are many resources to help churches think through this question, and to help everyone engage with reflection on all that the Eucharist can mean.[100]

Noticing and understanding people, smiling at them on encounter, thinking through the language and space we use are all important parts of evaluating how we truly see children and young people as part of the church, fully including and welcoming them to every part of our lives. But there was

---

100  Harding, Nick and Millar, Sandra, *Ready to Share One Bread: Preparing Children for Holy Communion*, London: SPCK, 2015.

one really practical action that emerged from the Life Events research with families, and it can be transformative in terms of seeing children and families extending their connection from one visit to many. As one parent expressed it: 'We always have good intentions of going to church but somehow life just seems to take over ... Which is quite sad ... As I do feel it's an important part of their lives. The church didn't keep in touch with us either.'

It is that last phrase that turns out to be crucial. We asked parents in different ways why they don't return to church, and I often ask church leaders to guess the answers when we meet at training events. They will often guess reasons like time, lives that are too busy, church being seen as unsuitable for children, but very few guess the number-one reason given, which is quite simply that they weren't asked or given any information. Keeping in touch is a vital part of welcome, and is now an everyday expectation from those we make contact with, whether a club, a charity or a gym. Organizations keep in touch, letting us know what they offer, what is going on and how we can get involved with them. All of this has to be done responsibly in line with GDPR, but once we are emailing people, then that contact can continue until the recipient decides they don't want to hear from us again.

One of the great blessings of living in the twenty-first century is that it has never been easier to be in contact with people – and contact is the soil in which relationships can grow. Consistently across all our research, whether about weddings, funerals or christenings, we found that nine out of ten people would like to hear from church again. Sadly, fewer than one in ten actually do. This is part of welcome too – building a relationship with good information and clear next steps to take.

This kind of transformation won't come easily. It might be painful and involve asking some hard questions with answers that are unexpected. Sometimes it might mean making some decisions that have a big impact, but the good news in this book is that it is often the details that start the process of change. It is thinking about our notice boards and our greetings, our words and our worship, so that our churches become places where children are truly welcome and God's people together experience a unity that transcends ages and generations.

# Appendix 1

# 'Home Sweet Home'

As part of my interviews with children, I used some of the techniques from Lego Serious Play[101] to explore what belonging and home meant to them. I found the results to be illuminating and useful in directing my thoughts on how church can be a place where they are welcomed, belong and feel at home.

They were told the purpose of the exercise and that the results would be used in a book, so they were aware they were making something that would be public. I had a variety of materials, including Lego, available, and gave them 12 minutes to make something that represented, to them, what it felt like to be at home and belong, somewhere.

We then took it in turns to look at each one. The person who made it had a chance to explain it to us, uninterrupted. We could then ask questions – the questions had to be open (ideally not yes/no answers) and about the model itself.

Unfortunately, the children included are all ten and up – two children aged six and eight were due to be included but at the last minute had a schedule conflict.

---

101 https://en.wikipedia.org/wiki/Lego_Serious_Play – I was trained by Ben Mizen of Ideas Alchemy (www.ideasalchemy.net/), who is the former children's and youth advisor to the Diocese of Portsmouth.

All five participants have been regularly attending the same church for at least the last eight years, so they have significant experience of being part of a church community and are relatively literate in terms of biblical and liturgical imagery and symbolism.

Here are the results.

# Mary, aged 16

**Mary**    On the left side – there's unity, diversity, love, because God is peace, and love, and then you've got the barrier, and on the right side you've got temptation, death, social climbing (people on the ladder), social media, the class divide. These are gravestones – representing fear of death. On this side you have immortality, going to heaven, being rewarded, and this side you have the fear of death, how everything comes to an end, and destruction.

**Me**      Can you explain what it is about the left side that makes you feel at home or like you belong there?

| Mary | Because everybody has a place. Everybody can belong here if they want to. Everybody has a place. There's nothing stopping you from being who you want to be and doing what you want to do – class divides can often create stereotypes and barriers, in terms of getting jobs, and good education, but in the good side of the world you have none of that. Everyone is equal, has equal opportunity and is respected in the same way. It's kind of unrealistic, but ... (*clearly struggles for the word*) |
|---|---|
| Me | But it's aspirational? |
| Mary | Yeah. |
| Me | So what is it that made you decide to put the picture of the church on that good side of this picture? |
| Mary | Because what the church does in the communities, and what it preaches in terms of forgiveness and loving and helping others is very good. I think faith is a good thing in that it gives people hope and communities. When you're feeling sad, or if there's something on your mind, you can come to church, or you can pray, and sometimes that will help you. |
| Jess | Why did you put the black line in the middle? |
| Mary | I wanted there to be colour and happiness on this side. |

## Wren, aged 10

| Wren | So this is a house. This guy's me, I've got some money (*the Playmobil figure is holding a coin*), and I feel peaceful around nature, and in the night, so this is fishies and a sharkie, and that's a salmon. |
|---|---|
| Matilda | Diversity in fish! I like it. |

**Wren**      This is my house. I feel peaceful and colourful. It has brick walls. They're safe. I was going to add in family but I didn't find any people. So this shooting star represents exploring and being everywhere. It's sort of peaceful and a happy place.

**Mary**      What do the triangles on the roof represent?

**Wren**      I just like lots of things made into one big thing.

**Mary**      I like how colourful your house is. It's like stained glass.

**Wren**      All the colours – red is death, but happy death. Blue is sea, green is nature, and yellow's food. If I see a brick wall, I just feel happy.

**Me**        They keep you warm, if you're inside.

**Wren**      The money – it represents, not much, but enough.

# Matilda, aged 14

**Matilda**    I thought, belonging is all about love. So home is all about being surrounded by people, people who also have love, which I demonstrated by giving them hearts. Some people have two hearts because I made extra. So this *(gestures to the tiger)* is the main person, and I feel like everyone here makes you feel so big. They big you up and make you feel good about yourself. So that's why they're really big. I gave them heart eyes *(not visible in the photo – the tiger has paper hearts on its eyes)* because they also love back, it's like a quid pro quo.

**Wren**    So they look and see love.

**Matilda**    That's exactly it. And this blanket represents the blanket of trust and how they're covered in trust, with all these lovely people, and there's a heart on it, because love is reflected in every piece and every aspect.

These chairs are a bit like Wren's brick wall – they surround them and make them feel safe. And I feel like I've really shown diversity in the chairs, there's so many different things which are protecting you, so many different ways.

**Mary**     But in a way, isn't that like you're not letting people in to enjoy this love?

**Matilda**  It's not like that. These are chairs of protection. It's very easy leaving the love and turning to hate. They're stopping people from leaving the love and turning to hate. There's lots of gaps, so people can get in.

**Delilah**  What does the tiger symbolize?

**Matilda**  It's something that we think is so scary but really isn't. And nature as well. And interconnectedness with nature. There's soooo many metaphors in my piece.

Protection, love and trust.

# Delilah, aged 12

**Delilah**  This picture is – this is the family – and you're always at home with your family. You always feel at home with your family. And you're kind of at home at church. And you're at home in nature, where you came from. And then we have love, because you love your family. And then we just have the sky. You feel at home with the people you know.

**Me**       So what is it about church that does or doesn't make you feel at home in this picture?

**Delilah**   I know all of you people from church. So you normally meet people at church that you wouldn't meet otherwise, so it's a place of community where you feel at home then, because you're with God, and with people you know. And nature – everything came from nature, nature is your home, you live in nature. And then your family.

That's dad, that's adopted son, that's mum, that's baby.

**Me**   Why did you choose to put in an adopted kid?

**Delilah**   I just couldn't find any other figure (with a skin colour that matched the parents). I think they might be gay – I'm not sure if the mum figure is a boy or a girl.

*This then descends into a discussion about adoption and surrogacy, and parthenogenesis in snakes.*

**Matilda**   *(indicating the figures by the trees on the left)* What are all these people doing?

**Delilah**   They're celebrating nature.

# Jess, aged 17

| Jess | So mine is a different approach – I thought we were doing different aspects of metaphorically looking at life, so it was kind of the idea – this is safety. Whatever life throws at you, if you have people to support you, you can get through it. So universal love … it's a nice idea, but unrealistic. But whatever happens, someone will be there to support you. |
| --- | --- |
| Mary | But people aren't always there to support each other. |
| Matilda | Why are they hugging the structure? |
| Jess | They're scared. They're scared of falling off. |
| Matilda | I thought it was they were climbing to achieve universal love. |

| | |
|---|---|
| **Jess** | Oh, that's a good idea! But that's more about competition – and we're not going for competition. |
| **Matilda** | I don't feel like it is competition, though – did this man climb over this woman to get on to this spot? |
| **Jess** | That could be, like, someone's drive, ambition, like Macbeth. But that's diverging from our topic a bit. |
| **Me** | But this just shows how an artist can make something, and people can have all different interpretations of it, and it's all coming from the same thing. |
| | *Irrelevant discussion ensues about which figure represents Donald Trump.* |
| **Me** | So what's going on with these children down here? |
| **Jess** | I kind of regret this symbolism of children at the bottom, because I think children are more important, and youth is the future – but it's supposed to be the parents supporting the child. |
| | I think the idea of safety in a home is about the people. In any situation, if there's people supporting you, you can get through it. And this is about how people have weaknesses too. |

# Appendix 2

# Resource List

## Websites

The author's blog: http://stalbanscme.com.

Spiritual Child Network – the Facebook group and their website: www.spiritualchild.co.uk.

Godly Play: www.godlyplay.uk.

Diddy Disciples: www.diddydisciples.org/.

Amy Fenton Lee – for children with additional needs: www.theinclusivechurch.wordpress.com.

We All Belong – for additional needs: www.allbelong.co.uk/.

Worship Workshop: www.worshipworkshop.org.uk.

Flame Creative Kids: www.flamecreativekids.blogspot.co.uk.

Karen Ware Jackson – intergenerational worship and parenting: www.karenwarejackson.com.

Worshipping With Children – resources for children in church on all Sundays of the three-year Revised Common Lectionary cycle, plus articles, from the Revd Carolyn Carter Brown: www.worshipingwithchildren.blogspot.co.uk.

Faith in Homes: www.faithinhomes.org.uk/.

GodVenture: http://godventure.co.uk/.

Church of England Life Events research and resources on baptism:
For parents, godparents, guests: https://churchofengland-christenings.org/.
For church leaders: https://churchsupporthub.org/baptisms/.

The Revd Ally Barrett's blog, including lots of free hymns and artwork: https://reverendally.org/.

The Revd Mary Hawes's Pinterest boards: https://uk.pinterest.com/revmaryhawes/.

Prayer Spaces in Schools (not just for schools!): www.prayer-spacesinschools.com/.

Mustard Seed Kids resources for imaginative spiritual play (conflict of interest alert – the author's company): www.mustardseedkids.co.uk (Beulah Land feltboard materials used in Appendix 1 are available here).

For well-being – an anonymous forum to share struggles in ministry, as well as joys, and receive advice and support: www.sheldonhub.org.

# Books

## *Children's spirituality*

Bettelheim, Bruno, *The Uses of Enchantment: The Meaning and Importance of Fairy Tales*, London: Thames & Hudson, 1976.

Bunge, Marcia J. (ed.), *The Child in the Bible*, Grand Rapids, MI: Eerdmans, 2008.

Caldwell, Elizabeth F., *I Wonder … : Engaging a Child's Curiosity about the Bible*, Nashville, TN: Abingdon Press, 2016.

Fowler, James W., *Stages of Faith: The Psychology of Human Development and the Quest for Meaning*, new edition, San Francisco, CA: Bravo Ltd, 1995.

Jones, Gerard, *Killing Monsters: Why Children need Fantasy, Super-heroes, and Make-believe Violence*, New York: Basic Books, 2003.

Mercer, Joyce Ann, *Welcoming Children: A Practical Theology of Childhood*, St. Louis, MO: Chalice Press, 2005.

Nye, Rebecca, *Children's Spirituality: What it is and Why it Matters*, London: Church House Publishing, 2009.

Pritchard, Gretchen Wolff, *Offering the Gospel to Children*, Cambridge, MA: Cowley Publications, 1992.

Westerhoff III, John H., *Will Our Children Have Faith?* 3rd edition, Harrisburg, PA: Morehouse Publishing, 2012.

Worsley, Howard, *A Child Sees God: Children Talk about Bible Stories*, London: Jessica Kingsley Publishers, 2009.

## *Ministry and Worship*

Barrett, Ally, *Preaching with All Ages: Twelve Ways to Grow your Skills and your Confidence*, Norwich: Canterbury Press, 2019.

Beckwith, Ivy, *Postmodern Children's Ministry: Ministry for Children in the 21st Century*, Grand Rapids, MI: Zondervan, 2004.

Beckwith, Ivy and Csinos, Dave, *Children's Ministry in the Way of Jesus*, Downers Grove, IL: IVP, 2013.

Csinos, Dave, *Children's Ministry That Fits*, Eugene, OR: Wipf & Stock, 2015.

Edwards, Carolyn, Hancock, Sion and Nash, Sally (eds), *Re-thinking Children's Ministry in Churches: A Practical Guide*, London: Jessica Kingsley Publishers, 2019.

May, Becky, *God's Story* (available in three age ranges), Abingdon: Bible Reading Fellowship, 2016.

Munns, Mina, *We All Share: Exploring Communion with Under-5s*, Buxhall: Kevin Mayhew, 2018.

Millar, Sandra, *Worship Together and Festivals Together*, London: SPCK, 2012.

Orme, Rona, *Rural Children, Rural Church: Mission Opportunities in the Countryside*, London: Church House Publishing, 2007.

Pritchard Houston, Margaret, *There is a Season: Celebrating the Church Year with Children*, London: SPCK, 2013.

Rundell, Simon, *Creative Ideas for Sacramental Worship With Children*, Norwich: Canterbury Press, 2011.

Turrell, Jennie, *Pray Sing Worship: A Guide to Holy Communion for Children*, London: SPCK, 2011.

Withers, Margaret, *Mission-Shaped Children: Moving towards a Child-centred Church*, London: Church House Publishing, 2007.

Withers, Margaret, *Where Two Or Three …: Help and Advice for Churches with Few or No Children*, London: Church House Publishing, 2004.

## Change Management and Process

Kotter, John and Rathgeber, Holger, *That's Not How We Do It Here! A Story About How Organizations Rise and Fall – and Can Rise Again*, London: Portfolio Penguin, 2016.
A very accessible, easy to read book, using the story of a clan of meerkats in the Kalahari to discuss group dynamics, responses to threats, and organizational change.

Sinek, Simon, *Start With Why: How Great Leaders Inspire Everyone to Take Action*, London: Penguin, 2011.

Hamilton, Pamela, *The Workshop Book: How to Design and Lead Successful Workshops*, Harlow: Pearson, 2016.

# Television and Film

*Babies: Their Wonderful World*. BBC 2; www.bbc.co.uk/programmes/b0bt7v0j.

*Old People's Home for 4 Year Olds*. An amazing intergenerational experiment from Channel 4, with much to teach churches; www.channel4.com/programmes/old-peoples-home-for-4-year-olds.

# Appendix 3

# Contents of Themed Story Bags/Baskets for Imaginative Spiritual Play

These are just samples of what can be done – mixing Bible stories with non-fiction topic books and resources that allow for imaginative spiritual play that connects to the images and symbols of the story or festival. There is no right or wrong way to play with these toys, and children may find a variety of uses for them.

## Baptism

*This one is sometimes loaned out to families for the baptism candidate's older sibling to play with. It's also used in baptism preparation with toddlers, and available in the Pray and Play area regularly.*

- Doll with christening gown;
- Shell;
- Wooden dove;
- The Baptism Cube toy (www.chpublishing.co.uk/books/9780715143209/the-baptism-cube);
- Baptism candle.

# Pentecost

- Grimms wooden stacking flame toy;
- Fabric scarves in red, orange and yellow;
- Windmills;
- Copy of *The Day When God Made Church: A Child's First Book about Pentecost* by Rebekah McLeod Hutto (Brewster, MA: Paraclete Press, 2016);
- Copy of *A Windy Day in Spring* by Charles Ghigna (London: Raintree, 2015) (non-fiction book about wind);
- Stuffed dove;
- Globe 'stress ball' (squishy) to represent the whole world;
- Dove Montessori puzzle;
- Ideally you would have bilingual books about wind or fire, but I couldn't find any.

## Easter

- Jesus doll (the one from Hope Education is no longer available – there is a Hallmark one available that's significantly less creepy than many others on the market);
- Caterpillar and butterfly finger puppets (symbol of resurrection and transformation);
- Easter story book;
- Copy of *The Lion Book of Poems and Prayers for Easter* by Sophie Piper (Oxford: Lion Children's Books, 2014);
- Donkey puppet;
- Sheep puppet;
- Toy bread;
- Cup (wooden egg cups work as mini chalices).